PEARL DAVIS

SPIRITUAL WARFARE SCHOOL OF THE PROPHETS

Spiritual Warfare Training

SPIRITUAL WARFARE SCHOOL OF THE PROPHETS

Pearl Davis

Order this book online at www.trafford.com
or email orders@trafford.com

Most Trafford titles are also available at major online book retailers.

Printed in the United States of America.

ISBN: 978-1-4269-6639-2 (sc)
ISBN: 978-1-4269-6640-8 (e)

Trafford rev. 07/06/2012

 www.trafford.com

North America & international
toll-free: 1 888 232 4444 (USA & Canada)
phone: 250 383 6864 ♦ fax: 812 355 4082

This Book Is Dedicated to the body of Christ and to all the mighty warriors nation wide who answered the call, paid the price and stayed in the battle and those who fought a good fight and finished the course and are now waiting in glory for their rewards, such as Apostle Paul, John the Revelator, Billy Gram and Kathryn Kuhlman and the other faithful apostles and Prophets who are now resting in glory to receive their rewards, my mom a woman of God who has gone home, my four children, my family, my grandchildren, my great grand children and my generations to come.

ACKNOWLEDGEMENT

I give honor to God the Father the Son and the Holy Spirit who is the director of this book. I acknowledge and honor my mother, a woman of God who planted seeds of value into my life, the most precious seed I cherish forever, is the lesson she taught, how to become a virtuous woman. I also thank God for my spiritual mother and mentor, Rachel Benbow who is now with the Lord. I give thanks to the late BISHIP MCMURRY, who was my earthly teacher in the ministry. I thank BISHIP Noel Jones for his encouragement from the word of God. I am grateful for BISHIP TD Jacks whom I adopted for my spiritual daddy, thanks for encouragement me as a woman and a leader. I praise God for my family who are my supporters in strength and inspiration, my son Joseph Davis, you are a gift to me from God, thank you for your great support your inspiration and encouragement though the hard time, the pain and the tears. My spiritual daughters Desrie Jenkins and Marie Levie I love you and thank you for your support. A great man Nathaniel Andrews, now deceased, he was a supporter and a blessing. Minister partners, fellow workers and friends.

CONTENTS

INTRODUCTION
WARFARE TRAINING

The most dangerous thing for man to do is reject Christ, they are turning to every thing except Christ, they have found new gods such as drugs, alcohol sex, a woman, a man, lying, cheating, killing, wife abuser, child abuse incest, gangs, stealing, fornication Adultery, homosexual, lesbian woman with woman, men with men, night clubs, witchcraft, lovers of self more than God, war. Fighting, anger, suicide worshiping false gods, satanic worship, and let us not forget religion: men are going to space, planning trips to the moon now they are trying to get to the sun. man kind is completely out of control. mothers and daughters are in warfare, fathers and sons are in warfare, sisters and brother are in warfare, families are in warfare, church members are in warfare. The world is in warfare, the nation is in warfare. People are worshiping counterfeit gods to escape the reality of the truth, which is the true and only living God:

our worse enemy is ourselves and Satan. Those who are not born again are been controlled by the adamic nature, the nature of Adam which is the sin nature. Those of you who have not been born again, this is the invitation to receive Jesus as your personal Savior, your new birth releases you from bondage and bring you under the blood covenant of Jesus Christ. Satan is going to and foe seeking to whom he may devour, he Searches the heart and mind for weakness, and then he began his attack.

Satan is the author of confusion, he confuses the mind and manipulates the individual into a life style that is a danger to the soul. Satan plants the thought of lust in the mind and then, he plants the desire for action. Lust is acted out because of disobedience to God's word. the people of God are commanded to abstain from sinful desires, which war against the soul, God has given us the power to abstain from this spirit and to overcome. We are sent to pray for the sinners for their deliverance because they are not aware of demonic attacks: our prayer is that they might receive the power of God as a weapon against the enemy, we are to show them the way to the kingdom of God: Satan attacks the weak and brings them into bondage, he use individuals against them selves and against others to destroy, he then drives them into acting out things one never thought they were capable of doing. Satan has blinded the eyes of the sinner: Lord open their eyes so they may see.

Marriage And Sex

It seem as if married is a thing of the pass: the attitude now is let's live together for a while, we must know if we are compatible, after a few year and it does not work each of us go our way. marriage originated is a part of God's design for mankind between a man and a woman. Marriage is an honorable union. Satan has attacked the minds of this generation in believing you should have sex before marriage, Satan is a lie, God's plan, sex is for married people, he put his approval on sex within the married viouls:

sexual intimacy is God's design, creation as male and female was his plan. The husband is responsible to satisfy the wife sexually, and the wife is responsible to satisfy her husband. The Generation of humans have attemped to satisfy their hunger though sex. Sexual immorality is sinful and need to be avoided. The result of going against God's principles bring on deadly sex disease. The soul is seeking for satisfactory, the only true satisfactory come from God. He is the healer of the soul. Satan is a lie. God's word stands forever, Satan is defeated God shall always be exalted. God commands the believers not to be unequally yoked. God state in his word that believers should married only believers, Marriage for the believers are under the covenant of God. If a Christian marry an unbeliever, 1 COR.7:12, if any brother has a wife who does not believe, and she is willing to live with him, let him not divorce her, same for the wife: the unbelieving wife is sanctified by the husband, and the unbelieving wife is sanctified by the husband. But if the unbeliever departs let him depart; a brother or a sister is not under bondage is such cases, but God has called us to peace.

Materialism

Everybody is running after materialism. The desire for more material gain lead to a trap of destruction. People who want to get rich falls into temptation and into foolish and harmful desires that plunge men into ruin and destruction. A greedy man stirs up dissension, do not wear your self out to get rich have the wisdom to show restraint. Desires for riches can side tract an individual from their belief. A man's life does not consist in the abundance of his possessions. The love of money is the root of all kind of evil. Some people, eagle for money, wandered from the faith and pierced themselves with many grief.

Many people stores up riches for themselves, when they die they leave it all behind for some one else to enjoy. James 5:1-5 you rich people, weep and wail because of the misery that is coming upon you, your wealth has rotted and moth has eaten your cloths, your gold and silver is corroded. Their corrosion will testify you and eat up your flesh like fire. You have hoarded wealth in the last days, Look! The wages you failed to pay the workman who mowed your fields are crying out against you.

The cry of the harvesters have reached the ears of the Lord Almighty. You have lived on earth in luxury and self indulgence You have fattened yourself of the slaughter for the last day. those who are rich in this present world, do not put your hope in wealth which is uncertain. If your sister or brother come to you for help, and you can help them but turn them away, God said the Love of God is not in you.

Anxiety and worry

Anxiety and worry come from fear, Satan control these spirits, it starts in your mind. An anxious heart weighs a man down, don't be anxious about anything Satan uses anxiety,worry and fear to discourage you.

Eating Disorders

Your body belong to God and is the temple of the Holy Ghost. He live in you. If you destroy his temple, God will destroy you; for God's temple is sacred and you are that temple.

Past Memories

Turn your mind from triumphs and failure, do not dwell on the past, never look back, go forward, leave the past trouble behind you. The weapons we fight are not weapons of this world, they have divine power to demolish strongholds. We demolish arguments and every pretension that sets it self up against the knowledge of God, and we take captive every thought to make it obedient to Christ. Concentrate on what God is doing in the present and will do in the future.

Psychics, Occult, Satan

Satan uses demons in attempt to defeat the Christian. It will not work because we are covered in the blood of Jesus and fully dress in our armor God forbid any dealing with the occult. God is against any one who practices divination or sorcery, interprets omens. Engages in wichcraft, or cast spells or who is a medium or spiritist or consults the dead. Any one who does these detestable practices the Lord your God will drive out those nations before you. these practices, and all who practice them shall have their place in hell.

Trials And Suffering

Do not be surprised at the painful trials you suffering it is not strange, trials are to be expected and remind us of the suffering Christ endured. We are to rejoice because God will reveal his glory in us and to us and we shall be glad. Our suffering cannot be compared to the blessings God is going to reveal to us exceedingly abundantly and above all we can ask or think.

Vanity/ Apparel

Dress need to be modest, not elaborate or for show, Israel's woman were corrected for unbecoming dress, concentrate on inner beauty rather than outer beauty. God is looking for our inner beauty. The unfading beauty of a quite and of a gentle spirit, which is of great worth in God's sight. God is not against woman because we dress to look beautiful, he is looking for the inner beauty, the spirit, his spirit, the beauty of the Holy Spirit.

Widows

A widow can trust God for her care. Isaiah 46: 4, even to your old age and gray hairs I am he, I am he who will sustain you, I have made you and I will carry you, I will sustain you and Iwill rescue you. The Lord keeps the widow's boundaries intact. Biblical examples of the widow Naomi, Ruth 1:16, Ruth stayed with her mother-in-law, she taken care of her. Psalm 68: 5 Defender the widows: Tim. 5:16, if any believing man or woman has widows, relieve those who are really widows.

All Scriptures Are Inspired By God

The inspiration of this training is coming from God 2Timothy 3:16-17, All scripture is inspired by God, and is profitable for doctrine, for reproof, for correction, for instruction in righteousness. That the man God may be thoroughly equipped forevery work.

The school of prophet is taught by the Holy Spirit. God has chosen leaders from among the body of Christ to teach his people, after man has reached his limitation God bring us into the heart of his revelation where no man can go unless he is ushered in by the Holy Spirit, man is limited, God is unlimited. 1John 2:27, but the anointing which you have received of him abides in you need not that man teach you, the anointing teach you all things and is true and is no lie

The purpose of this book is to guide you in spiritual warfare and to reveal to you the true principles of Gods word in using spiritual strategy to win the battle: God's word is sharper than any two edge sword, cutting, pulling down and destroying the powers of Satan.

Habakkuk 2: 2, God inspired the prophet Habakkuk to write this chapter for instructions to you, write the vision and to make it plain, that he may run that read it. God's desire is that his word is made simple PS. 119: 130, the entrance of thy word gives light, it gives understanding to the simple. God's word is made easy for you to understanding. PS, 19: 7 The law of the Lord is perfect, converting the soul, the testimony of the Lord is sure, making wise the simple. Proverb 4:7 God inspired Solomon to write the book of wisdom: Wisdom is the principle thing and is very important in spiritual warfare: therefore get wisdom. Proverb 4:5 get wisdom get understanding.

To know wisdom and instruction, to perceive the word of understanding, to receive the instruction of wisdom. To give prudence to the simple, a wise man will hear and increase learning.

Matthew was inspired, Luke was inspired, John was inspired, Peter was inspired, Paul was inspired, Timothy was inspired, Joshua was inspired in Joshua 1:6 as he gave instruction in warfare, be strong and of a good courage; only be strong and very courageous, that you may to do according to all the law which Moses my servant commanded you; do not turn from it to the right hand or to the left That you may prosper where ever you go

Have I not commanded you? Be strong and of a good courage; be not afraid, nor be dismayed, for the Lord your God is with you wherever you go.

Ruth the great grand mother of David was inspired, Ruth 1: 16+17, she refused to leave her mother in law because she was of age, she said, entreat me not to leave you. For where ever you go I will go where ever you lodge I will lodge, your people shall be my people and your God my God.

Job's body was covered with sores but though his pain, the words he spoken was inspiration from God, all of my appointed time, I will wait until my change come. The lord give it and the Lord Take it away bless be the name of the Lord.

Ester Cha. 4, Ester disobeyed the king's law for the love for her people. She was inspired by God, she said if I perish I perish, I am going before the king.

Daniel Cha. 3, Shadrach, Meshach and Abednego, was inspired by God not to worship the image, God inspired them as they spoke, our God whom we serve is able to deliver us from the burning fiery furnace.

Daniel cha. 6, Daniel went against the king's degree and refused to petition any other God other than the true and living God, instead God inspired him to continue to pray three times each day, he was cast into the lion's den, the angels came and delivered him.

Act Cha 2, on the day of Pentecost, the people were mocking the disciples and said they were full of wine, God inspired Peter as he spoke, for these are not drunk as you suppose but as the prophet Joel has spoken and in the last days I shall pour out my spirit out on all flesh your sons and daughters shall prophesy.

John Cha.1, when they said to John who are you? God inspired him to say I am the voice of one crying in the wilderness make straight the way of the Lord.

God inspired Jeremiah: he became discouraged Because the people would not listen to him, he And said he would not preach any more, God inspired him, he said it's Like fire shut up in my bones.

Each of us are inspired by the Holy Spirit each and everyday of our lives to live, move and have our being. {Inspire} to breath into, to move or guide driving or supernatural influence. Exalting supernatural. To introduce into the mind.

Jesus was inspired by his father God, we are inspired by Jesus. Jesus said if it be thy will let this bitter cup pass from me, God inspired Jesus as he spoke nevertheless not my will but thy will be done: God inspires Paul in Act 22 As he commanded him to go to Damascus, God said, and you will be told what you are appointed to do, Paul was inspired by God to move by faith.

God inspires us though his word, encourages us each day of our lives to walk by faith, he promises us not to worry about the next day: Matt. Cha.6: 25.take no thought for tomorrow, he promised tomorrow has been taken care of: God inspires us not to worry about anything, but to walk by faith and not by sight believe not the negative but only the positive. Jesus inspires us to love our enemies and pray for those who despise us, and to trust him with all our heart, and lean not unto our own understanding: obeying the word of God is defeat for Satan.

WELCOME TO THE WAR

The first war started in heaven before the foundation of the world Revelation 12:7, and there was war in heaven Michael and his angels fought against the Dragon and the dragon fought and his angels fought and prevailed not neither was his place found any more, Satan was cast out of heaven and his angels were cast out with him.

Roman 12: 12, woe unto the inhabited of the earth and the sea for the devil, the devil is come down unto you having great wrath because he know he has but a short time. Rev. 12: 17, and the devil was wroth with the woman and went to make war with her seed which kelp the commandment of God We are the seed, Satan is angry with us and hate us because we are the children of God, he hate the children because he hate the father. We are the children of God:

The warfare will continue until Jesus come back and once again rule :

The battle goes on between God and Satan and between the church, God chosen us into the warfare battle in John 15:16, you have not chosen me but I have chosen you. God chose us before the foundation of the world, Ephesians 1:4. Jesus sent us, John 15:16, he said go. John 17:15, Jesus prayed for us. Eph. 6: 10-18, God equipped for the battle:

The earth is the stage, the world is the war zone and the arena is for battle you and I are the battlefield, there is an evil spiritual unseen world out there, a wicked kingdom of principalities and powers, a world influenced by an evil spirit, his name is Lucifer, his title is Satan: we were born for battle, weaned for war chosen to be soldiers and warriors.

Revelation 12:12, the devil is come down unto you, having great wrath because he know he has but a short time. The definition of wrath is violent anger, and{ rage} definition of rage is to be mad, uncontrolled anger.

THE EXISTENCE OF SATAN

God did not create devil, but a beautiful perfect super angel, he was perfect in all his ways till iniquity was found in him, he became proud in his heart lifted up. God gave the angels free moral agency minds that were free to think and reason the right of free choice.

Lucifer allowed his wisdom and perfection to fill him with vanity—with self-glory, self desire, he became envious of God's power, resented authority over him, he plotted with his angels to marshal them into an invading army, to invade the heavens of God to knock God off the throne of the universe. Lucifer's desire was to be God, for that reason he was no longer light bringer but now an adversary an aggressor, a competition, an enemy, the name Satan means adversary, his angles are now demons. The earth was created perfect, then it became chaotic as a result of rebellion, a third of the angles united with Satan and now they are on earth as demons.

The first Adam failed God

Satan's first attack was on Adam and Eve, which at that time was the first church. God gave the commandment to Adam, of every tree of the garden you may eat but of the tree of knowledge, good and evil you shall not eat, for the day you eat of it you shall die. The serpent deceived the woman and said, eat it you shall not die. She ate and gave some to her husband and he ate. God had given Adam a chance to sit on earth's throne and restore the government of God on earth, because of sin he rejected the opportunity: Adam sold us out to Satan. Gen Cha. 3, Adam's sin bought a curse on mankind. The consequences of Curses resulting from sin of doing what is forbidden.

To the serpent, you will crawl on your belly and eat dust
To the woman, in pain you shall bring forth children
To Adam, curse is the ground for your sake in the sweat of your
Face you shall eat bread till you return to the ground, for out of it you were taken and to dust you shall return.

The First Murder

Adam's first son Cain, committed the first murder on earth, he killed his brother Abel, which loosed the spirit of murder on to the earth:

The Reason For Satan's Anger he desired to be God, he is yet fighting for leader ship over the earth, his desire will never come to pass he was defeated at the cross. Psalm 24:1, the earth is the Lord's and the fullness thereof the world and they that dwell in it. And God has given Jesus power over heaven and over earth.

We clearly understand Satan will never be God. he is the god of this world with a little g, he and his demons are evil spirits, and can only operate though inhabiting human bodies to carry out their assignment on earth. Satan's plan failed, he was kicked out of heaven; he is not owner of the earth nor the world: God is controlling the entire universe:

The earth is the Lord's the fullness thereof the world and they that dwell therein. We know Satan's end is defeat, Rev. 20:10. Satan shall be cast out into the lake of fire and shall be tormented day and night.

God gave Satan the position as being the god of this world which is the system, the government, which governs and controls the financial system but God is still in Control, Satan can do nothing unless he get permission from God: The god of this world is a set up for God's purpose during the tribulation. The God of this world does not control us because we are not of this world, God chose us out of this world and into his kingdom, John 15: 19.

Because of Adams sin, mankind became the property of Satan and was bought into slavery, Satan was the slave master but now we are no longer his slaves nor his property, we have been bought with a price, the blood of Jesus, Satan is no longer our master, we are his master.

The falling angles {demons} has been assigned by Satan to oppose the will of God, Satan's influence has cause mankind to conduct themselves into all matter of sin, such as, murder, adultery, fornication, envying lasciviousness, Idolatry, witchcraft, hatred, variance, emulation, wrath, strife and sedition, hatred, child abuse, wife abuse, child molestation, family incest, drug and alcohol abuse, insanity, fighting, idolatry, witchcraft gangs, demons using humans to sell drugs to destroy one another.

Jesus The Second Adam Succeeded

Four thousand years later God stepped out of glory took on the flesh of Jesus Christ came down 42 generation and enter the great contest—the contest of the temptation on the mount, Satan tries to use the same strategy of temptation he used on Adam but he failed, Satan said to Jesus, if thou be the son of God turn these stone into bread, Jesus took out his sword of spirit and said, get thee behind me Satan, it is written thy shall not tempt the lord thy God, God and only God shall I worship. Jesus was obedient unto death, he sold out to his destiny, he was true to his purpose, he fulfilled his purpose and dies on the cross for us.

Monumental struggle which taken place in that dark domain, death took it's utmost to shackle in its grip, it was impossible for death to keep it's prey: Psalm 107: 16, says he broken he gates of brass and cut the bars of iron in sunder. He and Satan struggled, Jesus took the keys of death and hell from the devil, and said, I am he who live forever and was dead, behold, I am alive forever Amen.

Jesus said to Satan, I have the keys of hell and the grave. The door way of death was unhinged at the name of Jesus, a place of agony the bible said, his soul suffered. He suffered with the transgressors, he suffered in our stead. he suffered until in the mind of God the claim of eternal Justice were met, Christ conflict and triumph in the infernal regions.

When the claim of eternal Justice was fully discharged, Christ was justified in the spirit, we were made alive in the spirit. 1 peter, 3: 18 our spirits were completely cut off and separated from God, but God made it possible that our fellowship be restored to him though Jesus Christ.

When Christ was exalted we the church was enthroned with him: when Christ took his seat in heaven proved that Satan's devastation was thrown into bankruptcy, he was stripped of his legal authority and dominion and was also stripped of his weapons. When Jesus busted forth from that dark prison and ascended upon high, all believers were raised, and seated together with Christ, we who believe are identified with him in his resurrection and exaltation and enthronement.

The word of God says he that is joined unto the Lord is one spirit 1 Corinthians 6: 17, all things have been legally put under his feet. When Jesus conquered the forces of darkness, he left them disarmed before he rose from the dead, we who are believer were participants in the victory. When he snacked the keys of death and the grave from Satan and burst forth from that abyss, we were sharer in the trump, when he ascended up on high and took his seat in the heaven, we were exalted with him.

Satan and all his host of hell are beneath our feet, they are under our feet. When Jesus conquered Satan, we became Satan's master, he can no longer Lord over us, his dominion ended at Calvary, instead of him having power over us. we have been given authority over him. The word of God declares we are seated in heavenly places with Christ. Satan realizes we are his master, so he bluff the church in deception, he is aware of the fact that he has lost the battle.

The best he can do is to harass and sabot you. Satan sends demons to you to tire you out by persistent effort of attacks, to worry and annoy you. His purpose is to hinder and oppose the will of God. People of God the victory is already yours, God could have completely put Satan away but God has chosen him to give the church on the job training in spiritual warfare. We soon will take our place with Christ on the throne following the marriage supper of the lamb:

the crown belong to the conquerors. Without an adversary their could be no practice in overcoming, when Satan try to oppress us we must remember we have the authority over Satan, he is subject to us, we must remember we are in Christ and because of this, Satan cannot touch us, if you are held in bondage to demons of fear, sickness, diseases, it is because of your ignorance of your power in the blood of Jesus.

We have been delivered though the blood of Jesus from the power of the slave driver Satan. Jesus paid the price for our victory, and at the name of Jesus every knee shall bow and every tongue shall confess that Jesus is

Lord. 11 Corinthians 4: 3+4 The gospel is hid from them who are perishing In whom the god of this world has blinded the eyes so that they may not see the light of the gospel.

We soon will take our place with Christ on the throne following the marriage supper of the lamb, the crown belong to the conquerors. Without an adversary their could be no practice in overcoming, when Satan try to oppress us we must remember we have the authority over Satan, he is subject to us, we are in Christ and because of this, Satan cannot touch us, if you are held in bondage to demons of fear, sickness, diseases, it is because of your ignorance of your power in the blood of Jesus.

We have been delivered though the blood of Jesus from the power of the slave driver Satan. Jesus paid the price for our victory, and at the name of Jesus every knee shall bow and every tongue shall confess that Jesus is Lord.

Ephesians 1:7, We are redeemed though Jesus blood for forgiveness of sin according to his grace

Luke 22:20, likewise he also took the cup after supper, saying, this is the new covenant in my blood, which is shed for you. The Lord's supper is to remind us of the blood Jesus shed on the cross for us.

11 Corinthians 4: 3+4 The gospel is hid from them who are perishing in whom the god of this world has blinded the eyes so that they may not see the light of the gospel. John 6:54, whosoever eat my flesh and drink my blood has eternal life. Eating and drinking is used figuratively of partaking of the benefits of the death of Christ. We partake by faith and enjoy the benefits because God gives them on the basis of what Christ did for us. Eph. 2:8-9, Rom. 3: 24-25: 5; 1:11 10:9-10; Act 3: 16; 4:12; 15:9, 26:18; Gal. 2:16-20; 3:1-26; 1 Pet.1:5-13. John 53+54, believing on Christ is the same as eating and drinking him.

YOUR FIRST TRAINING IS BOOTH CAMP

* You will learn how to bring flesh under subjection
* You will learn to recognize demonic attacks in your flesh
* you will learn the secret of conquering your flesh.

Becoming an effective warrior you must conquer these enemies

* 1 John 2: 14-16, overcoming the wicked one
* Love not the world nor the things in the world.

Things in the world you must overcome

* Lust of the flesh
* Lust of the eye
* The pride of life

You are a spirit, you live in a body

Your body is made up of these parts
* mind
* soul
* will
* emotion

Your mind is the battle ground

Your mind is Satan's target

* Your flesh follows
* Your will follows
* Your emotions follows
* Your spirit follows

Roman 8: 7+8, Because the carnal mind is enmity Against God; so then they that are the flesh cannot please God, verse 13, he command us to modify the deed of the flesh. Those who are under the control of their old sinful nature, is bent on following their old evil desires and can not please God. But you are not like that. You are controlled by your new nature if you have the Spirit of God in you.

Three of the enemy territory you must conquer

* Fear Timothy 1: 7, God has not given us the spirit of fear
* doubt Mark 11: 23, if you do not doubt you shall have what ever you say
* worry, don't worry about anything pray about everything

Strategy of winning the war

* walk in obedience
* follow orders
* Remain focus

The most important of these strategy is obedience

Obedience is your entrance into spiritual warfare:

Philippians 2:8, obedient unto death, obedience is better than sacrifice

Job 36: 12, but if they obey not they shall perish.

Jeremiah 7: 23, but this is what I command them saying, obey my voice and I will be your God, and you shall be my people, and walk in my ways that I have commanded you that it may be well with you.

Jeremiah 12: 17, if they will not obey I will utterly pluck up and destroy that nation. God is preparing his church for a great outpouring of his holy spirit, he has chosen obedient disciples to carry out purpose.

SPIRITUAL WARFARE TESTIMONIES

Spiritual warfare was a life style for me, because I had to deal with the behavior of mental abuse from mom, because of the pain she carried, from brutal treatment she received from her mom and family members. My mom was a strong woman and I admired her for her strength, the ability to endure what ever life bought her way. Mom was a born again Christian, she loved God and was a believer in fasting and praying, many times I heard her calling my name out to God, I thank God for my mother's prayers, even thou she was not delivered from her pain of abuse but with a broken heart she taught me the value of becoming a virtuous woman and to have strength, courage and temperance: God loved mom and because of his mercy and loved he forgave her for her controlling and dominant ways.

Mom taught us the golden rule which I never forgotten, do unto others as you would have then do unto you. she was a woman of God and of faith, and taught to us the word of God. My mom taught me values I will never forget. which I treasure for a life time.

As a child mom never praise me no matter how hard I tried, my reward was criticized, now I understand, she could give only that which she had learned, the negative part of her was an empty well without water. The positive side of her was the God side which taught me the things of God and the values of life. Mom loved me and showed it in many ways, but being a child and a teenager at that time I did not understand, I felt emptiness with a lonely and unloved heart.

Whenever the memory of mom's childhood abuse appeared, I felt the pain of her criticism and her wrath of mental abuse. It continued to the point I was unable to endure. During that time the church was not aware of deliverance ministries or spiritual warfare. The saints loved God and were filled with the Holy Spirit, but they were bounded, many of them carried deep scars, hurts and lived with wounded spirits bitterness and unforgiveness. they shouted and praised God in denial of their pain. Mom did was not aware of the satanic forces behind her actions toward me: Satan was using her pain for my destruction.

My life at home with mom was stressful but I had no place to go. I was robbed of my self esteem, I became confused and lonely. Warfare was so bad at home I felt as if I was living with an enemy. It seem as if the devil followed me to school, I had to fight to protect myself at school from first grade to high school, the warfare was on I had no knowledge of fighting in the spirit during that time so I fought with my fist. warfare at home, warfare in school, warfare on the job. fist fighting and cursing was my protection.

Warfare In Marriage

The warfare continued. At that time I not aware of spiritual warfare. I did not have a clue God was preparing me for a spiritual warfare ministry. The age of fifteen one day walking home from school, I met a young man, he was twenty years of age, his conversation was inviting, he was nice to me and showed me much kindness, he walked me home from school everyday, we became inseparable, we thought we were in love, I shared with him my abuse at home with mom: one day he proposed to me and offered to take care of me, he and I took the ideal to mom, she was furious because I was only fifteen years of age, her idea for me was to finish school, which of course she was right, but this was my chance to get away. I ran away from home with him for two days: we received word that mom had called the police I went home, mom was angry and furious, she put me on a punishment, he was not welcome at our house. Mom and Dad knew my determination, they gave he and I permission to marry. The reason was, they did not want me to become pregnant before marriage. My mom signed for me to marry. So we were married.

We were find for a while and then all hell broke out, I was taken on another abuse journey, this journey was not only mental abuse but both mental and physical abuse. Warfare in my marriage I had gone from bad to worse. I found out later that my husband was raised in a broken home by his mom without a father, his dad left his mom after he was born. Afterward his mother married a man who constantly Abuse her. Later I found out my husband had a bad temple plus he was jealous: he had a job and was a good provider but I was being abused often. I was in pain, heartbroken, sad and confused. I believe his attitude would have been better if had his dad been in his life. My husband continued to abuse me, one day I took my daughter and left, we ended up in divorce Being young, divorced, and single life was hard, it seem as if Satan loose every demon in hell loose on me.

I have been abused mentally, physical, abused by church folk, abused by sinners, shot at, terrible car accidents, rejected, disappointed persecuted, deceived, lied on, lied to, hated, left alone, sick and healed, homeless, broke, broken, wounded broken spirit, deceived, heartbroken, but now God is blessing me exceedingly abundant and above all I can ask or think: God has restored everything the enemy has stolen. I am blessed going and I am blessed coming, I am blessed in the city and in the field. Even thou I am blessed but many times I had to walk alone, sometimes friendless, lonely and single, some time discouraged, some time happy, some time sad, some time up and some time down, but as a warrior I've had to endure the things life bring, but though it all God has made me to triumph and has always brought me out victorious. I remember the Paul words in Philippians 4:11, I have learned in whatsoever state I am in be content, I know how to be abased and I know how to be abound, I am instructed both to be full and hunger, to abound and to suffer need.

The battles have been hard but now I realize God was preparing me for this ministry from childhood. God has given to me his conquering power over every battle and has always brought me out a winner. The journey has been hard and lonely, but the price paid for the anointing is worth the pain.

Generational Curse destroyed

The abuse with my mom was a generation curse, God showed me it had to be broken, but first I had to forgive her and love her in spite of the abuse. God led me into my deliverance, thought much fasting praying and tears, the Holy Spirit took me though the deliverance: Jesus held me and loved me all the way though my deliverance. Going through my deliverance was like a drug addict being delivered from drugs, the pain was severe, much pain, and many tears, the scars, the wounds, the hurt, my wounded spirit, my broken heart, years of being rejected. No one knew I was paining to be delivered, but I stayed with God until deliverance came. After some years God delivered me. O what a joy. I was delivered and free.

I prayed to God, help me never to have that attitude toward my daughters, God answered my prayer; I love my daughters and always wanted them to know I loved them, I never wanted them to feel insecure or rejected The generation curse has been broken, it stopped with me. I have two daughters, seven granddaughters and one great granddaughter, I love them dearly and they love me: I thank God for His blessings. **You who have experienced family abuse, it must stop with you, the generation curses must be broken: The generation curse can only be broken though fasting and praying**.

God used me to lead my three brothers and my father to God before their death: before mom died, I led her though the deliverance prayer, she was delivered from bitterness and unforgiveness, she was forgiven. My three brothers was drugs and alcohol addicted. My younger brother was on his death bed in the hospital, I led him into the sinner's prayer, and he received Christ at the last hour. He was free to go to his heavenly home. About three years ago. God showed me he was going to take my oldest brother, I called him every day and ministered to him, the third days before he passed I led him into the sinners prayer, he was free to go to his heavenly home. My father was raised up in

Church he loved church and attended regular, he sang in the choir and worked in the office of a deacon, He was a good man and tried to treat his fellowman right. I thought he was saved, he was sick with old age, one day he said to me I want to be saved, I led him into the sinner's prayer, God saved him and he was free to go to his heavenly home. many people in the house of God are dedicated in serving but are in need of salvation, This area need addressing in the house of God, the people must understand their works will not get them into heaven only salvation will get them in the door of heaven.

Many years ago my daughter became a drug addicted, she was a back slider; but I refused to give her up, I went into spiritual warfare, laid before God in fasting prayer and faith, God delivered her and gave her a job in a drug rehab as supervisor, now she is a witness to others that God is a deliverer.

About twenty years ago one night a man came into my house through a window, and woke me up with a knife at my throat, my children was asleep, I was frighten but I did not panic, I began to say the blood of Jesus, the man dropped the knife and ran out of the house. The blood of Jesus saved my life.

The year 2000, two sisters and I had left church, after taking them home I parked on the side walk to let them out, coming toward us was two gang members walk up to my car pointing a shot gun at me, cocked and ready to shoot, he said to me what is your business here, about a month earlier God had ordered me to carry a bible in the windshield of my car, I reached for the bible and said, Jesus is my business, the young man let down the shot gun turn around and they went back the way they came.

Years ago my son was on his way to the store, I was inside of the house, I ran outside, I saw about ten boy jumps on him, they had him down on the ground. They drew back their fist to beat him, I yelled Jesus, the blood of Jesus, all of a sudden, the boys jumped off him they looked around as if they saw something, on their faces were fear and they fled, I believe they saw angels. I am a witness that God is faithful.

One afternoon, I left work and was on my lunch break, as I was passing by a barber shop, a ride by shooter Shot at the barber shop, As I dropped to the ground I felt the breath of the bullet about an inch from my face it passed me and shot a man in the barber shot. Again God saved my life, the word of God states; I shall not die but live and declare the word of the Lord. I am declaring the word of God now. God's word is true and is not a lie, his word shall not return unto him void but shall accomplish his purpose.

I arrived in California the year 1969; my first job was house work. One day as I walked across a large field on my way to work, I heard dogs barging behind me; two Doman pigeon killer dogs were viciously running behind me. I was a new convert and was taught to use the blood of Jesus on demons. Fear gripped my heart but I was not able to move, I stood still, pointed at them and constantly repeated the blood of Jesus. They came near me and slid as a car would slide on brakes; they turned back and ran the way they came, howling as if they had been hit with a big rock. I'm a witness there is Power is in the blood of Jesus.

My children and I was riding in the car with my mom one afternoon as she Drove the 110 freeway, all of a sudden the tire and brim came off her car, the car spin three times on the freeway it turned upside down and began sliding on the freeway, we were looking at the top of the car, I was yelled Jesus, Jesus, Jesus, God helped mom control the car and bought it back in order, no one was hurt and no collision Accident. This was a miracle; God's angles were there to help us. God declared in his word, he has encamped angels around us. Thank God for the blood, which is the greatest weapon given to us to use in spiritual warfare.

Years ago I was driving to Bakersfield to run a revival, as I was driving though the Grape vine on the freeway, a terrible rain wind storm arose, it seem as if the wind would blow my car away, as I drove around the cliff, I could barely see, as the rain and wind began to beat against the wind shield. God was in control because my view was shallow I wasn't able to see anything, but I kelp driving around the cliff, I began praying and called on the name of Jesus. Suddenly out of nowhere appeared bright lights the spirit of the Lord said, follow the lights, I believe the angles came to guide me out, after I was led off the freeway the lights disappeared.

I woke up one morning there were a large thing hanging on my neck even though I had faith, I was frightened, I constantly went to the doctor but they had no answer, one day the doctor said they were going to operate and take it off, I said no, God is going to heal me, I went home fell on my knees and cried out to God, he spoke to me and said, fast three days and three nights, I am going to heal you. I obeyed God. The night of the last part of the fasting, God put me into deep

Spiritual sleep, though my healing process I felt heat moving though my neck. I felt heat moving though my neck but not able to wake up, early the next morning my bed shook as if someone was shaking it. The spirit of the Lord said, go look in the mirror, the thing had disappeared, I was healed. Obedience and faith is powerful. John Cha. 9, the man was born blind, Jesus spat on the ground and made clay with saliva and anointed the blind man with clay and said go and wash in the pool of Siloam, the man obeyed and came back seeing.

The year 1994, I was driving on my way to work, depressed and discouraged. I began to think on all the hard test and trial I had gone though and they continued it was as if they would never end constant warfare. I felt tired and burn out. I thought in my mind, Lord if you are not going to bless me take me home. All of a sudden a big van out of nowhere ran into my car, a terrible crash, my car ended up in side of the side of his van, my head hit the dash board, I was in great pain and was not able to move, the spirit of the Lord spoke to me and said, I heard you thinking, I am giving you a choice if you are ready to go home I will take you now, at that time an angel appeared, he was very tall, he was in white and had huge wings, he stood between my car and the van which was wrecked.

I was completely out, but my spirit was aware of this spiritual event that was taking place. I heard the word of the Lord, I shall not die but live and declare the work of the Lord, I repeated those words, and I shall not die but live and declare the works of the Lord. As soon as I spoke those words the angel disappeared. And then I heard the spirit of the Lord say, it is not your time; your work is not finished. At that moment I felt strength coming into my body, my fingers began to move, I slowly began moving my head, and I looked up and saw my car inside of the van. I leaned against the door and it opened, I believe the angel of the Lord opened the door; otherwise it would have been impossible for me to get out. I heard people from afar off. As I began crawling out of the car, I said somebody call 911. I was taken to the hospital, after my exam, the doctor said, I was little shaken up but find. It's amazing how God stop stopped every thing during the spiritual process. God is in control of every situation in our lives. Satan cannot touch us unless he gets permission from God. God created the devil and uses him for his purpose in training us: after we have conquer different areas of warfare, God commands Satan back off until the next test,

The enemy was trying to take me out but God kelp me alive for my purpose. I thank God for a purpose, without a purpose human life has no meaning and make no sense. Our purpose is to carry out God's desire. Whatever we are called to do, we must fulfill our purpose and destiny. God has given me another chance: I am grateful and I am running for my life.

During my season of my testing, I became homeless, I lost almost everything, I was left with my car, clothes and my bible. I was homeless during those times God taught my hands to war; I did not retreat in the time of battle. I continued in church, working on my post and never ceased to praise God. I used my spiritual weapons and believed God for deliverance: I trusted him forever.

He was my very help in the time of trouble. I slept in my car for two years; MCDONALD was my table and bath place for hygiene purposes. After the two years, l lived in a mission after that, I slept in a church on a hard beach. The entrance to the church was in the back, every day and night dope addicts gathered in the back of the church, I had to go threw them to go inside the church, God was my protected. After a few months God inspired me to conduct a revival at the same church, many were healed and set free. Afterward, God provided for me decent place to live.

Territory Restored

About twenty years ago God assigned me to take back territory from Satan, during that time I was a single parent providing for my children. I was seeking God for a larger house for my children. I found a four bedroom house for rent. I did not like the house nor the neighborhood but the rent was four hundred a month which was a reasonable price. The house and the neighborhood were written in gang language. My children opposed the ideal. I obeyed God and moved into the house which had been empty for about three years, because of fear of the gang; they had taken over the neighborhood which caused the people to fear.

The same night gangs intruded and settled in the back of the house outside, after we had gone to bed, we heard shooting at the house; we fell to the floor until the shooting stopped: the next day I went on a fast, God spoke to me and said, I'm going to use you to take back this territory. He said I will protect you and your children and I have encamped angels around you and your children to protect you.

The next day the children and I cleaned off the gang language from off the house. The gangs watched and smoked their drugs: many days and nights ride by shooting would occur but God protected us and gave me peace. My children and I continued going church and doing our daily routine without any interference. God led me on a fast he spoke to me said, move all the furniture to the back, I know the voice of God so I obeyed. Then he said, make this part of the house a church: I was confident this was the voice God. I was called to run a revival, I prophesied to a young man who needed a job, He called me a few days later and said he had received a Job, a preacher had given up his church and left all the church furnisher, he brought the furnisher to me and placed every piece in its proper place. God provided everything I needed to start the church, people came from everywhere, the gangs came, and many of them were saved and delivered.

They cleaned up the neighborhood from the gang language and left the neighborhood, the people was once safe again. God moved me and my children out of the neighborhood into a better place. I have learned though experiences seasons for our lives are panned by God.

Victory over Satan territory

During the year 1970, Satan captured my daughter and took her on a long trip of slavery into the addicting of drugs, he also attacks my sons and my other children, the fight was on, and the Holy Spirit led me into battle against the Rulers of darkness. God led me into Satan's territory and delivered out my children from the hands of the enemies.

People of God you must fight for your children, go in faith deliver them out of the hands of the enemy. You have the power. God said do not Fear he is with you: This kind of warfare challenges you into fasting and praying, these demons are stubborn, these come out only by fasting and praying.

Warfare in the House of God

Coming from a history of abused and rejection, I was a broken, hurting low self esteem, mentally confuse, seeking for love and comfort; my view was, everybody in the house of God was saved. And their arms of protection would embrace me, I walked in the house of God with confident and assurance I would find love. I went in looking for refuge but instead I found disappointment, I found myself in warfare in the house of God.

I enter into another battle on another level. My real battle had just begun. Little did I know this battle would determine my victory or defeat in going to the next level into my purpose. I found out, those who rejected Christ were used by Satan to abuse the people of God.

Being a baby saint I had no church knowledge but as I continued to study God's word, I gain knowledge that Satan had assigned his demons to the house of God. These demons are angels of light and Satan ministers, they recognized my identity and the anointing and began their attack. My warfare in the house of God was with spiritual wickedness in high places and principalities. Fasting and prayer was food for survival. I was wounded in the house of God. Zech.13: 6, David said, I was wounded in the house of my friends. Many of us can identify with this pain, but it was just a test, now move on to the next level, and whatever is next that too shall pass.

Wolves in Sheep Clothing

The word of God came to me saying Matt. 10: 16, behold I send you forth as sheep in the midst of wolves, be wise as serpents and harmless as doves. Wolves in sheep clothing are the abusers in the house of God. I needed questions to many answers. Prayer and fasting was my meat. God spoke to me in Ephesians cha 6, we wrestle not against flesh and blood but principality, powers, the rulers of darkness of the world, spiritual wickedness in high places, these are our opponents. Satan has transformed his angles into angles of light, they are responsible for the actions in the house of God, and they are assigned to bring division into the house of God. In this book you will find answers to many questions the information from this book will equip you to do spiritual battle.

The anointing was the key weapon for my deliverance, during my season of testing, many storms rose in my life. I lost almost everything I was left with my car, a few clothes and my bibles, for the first time in my life I became homeless. During my season of testing God taught my hands to war. My life style was steadfast in fasting and prayer which ushered me into the anointing which destroyed the yokes of the enemy, Faith helped me to hold on to God's promises I held on with the weapon of endurance which helped me to stand and the word of God sustained me. God is faithful, he restored things back Satan had stolen. We all must learn to endure hardness as a good soldier.

My years of my training were tough, but God helped me to endure hardness as a good soldier. After being taught under the direction of the Holy Spirit, he put on my head a spiritual cap which is the helmet of salvation and he covered my body with a gown, which is the spiritual amour of God. Ephesians 6:12. God put Joshua in training under the leadership of Moses for years, when his training was over he came forth as a mighty and powerful man of God. His faith conquered all. Whatever test God has purposed for your life, go though, I'm a witness, and God will bring you out. Roman 8:17, but he shall endure to the end, the same shall be saved, if so be that we suffer with him we shall be glorified together with him. I have gone though many hard test but God comforted me in them all.

God uses suffering to stir sharing among the believers. Believers who suffer are not to become self centered, bitter, discouraged, apathetic nor are the believer to become complaining, they are to allow God to comfort them. This should be the hope and expectation of every believer, God expect you to suffer with the right attitude and he expect us to share his comfort, as I am sharing with you in this book,

Ps. 23: 4, thy rod and thy staff they comfort me.
Ps 71: 21, he comforts me on every side.
Ps 119: 50, this is my comfort in my affliction.
Isaiah 51:3, The Lord shall comfort Zion
La. 2: 13, I may comfort O virgin daughter

2 Corinthians 1:3, of mercies and of God of all comfort
Ephesians 6: 22, and that he may comfort your heart
Roman 1: 12 that I may be comforted
2 Corinthians 1:4, wherefore we ourselves are comforted

Col. That their hearts might be comforted God comfort us in all our tribulation, that we may be able to comfort those who are in any trouble, with the comfort which we ourselves are comforted by God,

2 Corinthians 1:4. The word tribulation mean to be weighed down, to be pressed and crushed, God comfort you so you can comfort others God carries you through trials so that you can strengthen and comfort others.

GOD SHOWED ME A VISION

In this vision I saw God people being attacked by a multitude of demons, they fell to the ground with a loud scream, after that I saw another vision of people behind bars, they reached out as I passed the screams were for help, the voices were a cry for deliverance. I saw people running to and fro in confusion, I heard voices is there a word from the Lord? People foaming at the mouth, hands reached out, voices crying help me, I saw people dressed up in fancy suits and clothing walking pass the helpless people: I heard voices crying out, does anybody care. I saw young people jumping up and down, dancing but in their hearts they were crying out, help me, I need deliverance, help me, show me how to be like Jesus, show me how to live holy, don't agree with me when I am wrong but please, show me the right road to travel. God showed me in this vision young woman dress in street clothes, half naked dancing like a snake. Needles hanging from their arms, cigarette hanging from their mouth, infected with drugs and alcohol, they appeared to be having a good time, but I heard their hearts crying out, help me. Somebody help.

God's words to me, I'm commanded you to Go and set the captive free. God spoke to me and said, I have led you into battles against the powers of darkness, I bought you though great victory with the experience of a great warrior, you have been tried in the fire and now, you shall come forth as pure gold tried in the fire.

God said, tell my people, my ministers, my leaders and the body of Christ, Give word to my people those who has a covenant with me, tell them to repent I will forgive them: it's time to go, The harvest is ripe waiting to be picked, souls are waiting: God said, I wish you were hot or cold, those of you who are luck warn he said, I will spit you out of my mouth.

God's word to me, I have trained, taught and assigned you to go in the power of my might and deliver the people, cast out demons from those who are bound. Tell my people, they made a vow to work in the vineyard, they turned, no one is in the field, tell them to repent and get back on the Job, otherwise I will hold those responsible for the lost souls who are on their way to hell, God said tell them they will stand before me at the judgment and they will be judged, God said, go teach the people spiritual warfare spiritual strategy though my word and how to use their spiritual weapons skillfully. I remembered sitting up in the bed and revisited my pass of tests trials and victories God has given me, my face was filled with tears, I began to praise but I felt unworthy and unqualified for the task. He said, I have qualified you for the Job.

Now I understand the reaction of Moses when he received his assignment from God, his reply, who am I that you should send me, my words were, Lord make me worthy, the anointing came over me, I said yes Lord and began worshiping God, I heard the voice of the Lord say, I'm assigning you to write a book, call it spiritual warfare school of the prophets: I will instruct you in writing the book. his anointing filled the room where I was sitting, I and said, yes Lord.

The vision has become reality and is now in operation, I am working in my purpose: though this ministry the word is being preached, demons are cast out, the sick is being healed, the captive is being set free. I thank God for the anointing on my life and in this ministry. Then Peter began to say unto him, see, we have left all and followed thee. Mark 10:28, whosoever that forsaken not all cannot be my disciple. Jesus said, there is no one who has left houses, brothers, sister, father or mother or wife or children or land, for my sake, who shall receive a hundred now in this time with persecution and eternal life.Ye are my witness, said the Lord my servant whom I chose: that you know believe and understand that I am he: none is before me nor will be after me.

Winning Lost Souls

Luke Cha.8, after Jesus has spoke to the multitude, he said, he who has an let him hear. His disciples asked, what does this parable mean? Jesus said, to you it has been given to know the mysteries of the kingdom of God, but to the rest it is given in parables, that seeing that they may not see, and hearing they not understand.

Proverb 11:30, The fruit of the righteous is a tree of life, he who win souls is wise. In winning souls you must have genuine love, otherwise they will flee from you, sinners know if you are fake, most of them are from the street and have experienced of fake, now they seeking for love and refuge and are searching for the anointing to make them free. After they have come into the house of God, they are seeking for the truth: God has chosen us to teach them his way and his principles, God will hold us accountable for his souls.

1 Corinthian Cha. 3, For you are still carnal, for where There are envy, strife, and division among you, are you not carnal? and behaving as mere men? For when one say, I am of Paul, and another say, I am of Apollo's, are you not carnal? Who then is Paul I am of Apollo's, and who is Apollo's, but ministers through whom you believed as the lord gave to each one? I plant, Apollo's watered, but God who gives the increase. So then neither is he who plants anything, nor he who water, God who gives the increase.

Now he who plants and he who waters are one, and each one will receive his own reward according to his own labor. God's plan for the church is that we join together with the spirit of God all having mind and one purpose, winning soul out of the hands of Satan and into the kingdom of God. This strategy defeats the power of Satan, because where there is unity there is strength. And now we can enter into the enemies camp together pull down his strong holds and pull out souls for Christ. You must target the enemy know his strategy and recognize his place, you must have knowledge of the magnitude and extent of the war, this task calls for spiritual warfare training. the holy spirit will show you the enemies plans, which will allow you to go into Satan's territory to bring out the captive and let the oppressed go free.

No human is able to save a soul,

the Holy Spirit the qualified one for this job. God has chosen us as instruments to bring forth his work, our bodies are his instruments to work though, our bodies are the temples of the Holy Spirit, he work though us to get his job done: every test is assigned by God to bring our lives into fruitfulness: every victory won brings in the anointing which is required for winning the lost: the anointing destroys the yokes, demons are cast out the individuals are set free. 2Corinthians,1:20, now he who establishes us with you in Christ and has anointed us is Christ, who has sealed us and given us the spirit in our hearts as a guarantee.

Luke 9:6, so they departed preaching the gospel and healing every where. Act Cha. 3, The lame man who was lame from his mother's womb laid daily at the gate asking alms, peter and John was anointed men of God said silver and gold have I none but in the name of Jesus rise up and walk. Though the anointing of God the man walked. The anointing of God destroys the yoke and set him free. Many today are sitting in the house of God demon possessed. They are in need of deliverance only the power of God can set them free. Mark 16:17, and these signs shall follow you. I pray for the anointing of God to return back into the house of God.

In my name they shall cast out demons. Mark 5, Jesus met the man coming out of the tomb, with an unclean spirit, no man could bound him even with chain, he was mad, he would cut himself with stone Jesus said, come out you unclean spirit, he cast the spirit out and sent them Into the swine; people went to see the man who had been mad, he was cloth in his right mind.

Be Aware Of These Weapons

Satan come to kill, steal and destroy your hope and your faith, these weapons are aimed at your purpose.

Jealousy In The House Of God

Hosea 4: 6, my people are being destroyed for the lack of knowledge lack of [information] your information is in the word. study to show yourself approved unto God: after God approves you, your heart approved though repentance and obedience. Only then will God delivered you from the spirit of Jealousy, which qualifies you to enter into the battle. And now you are ready

For spiritual warfare, Isaiah, 58:6, to do the heavy burdens and let the oppressed go free. Satan strategy is to destroy the unity with in the body of Christ, he has planted a strong hold of Jealous among the members and the leaders of God which must come down. The true church has the power to destroy Satan's power which he has planted among the body and the leaders. God's word said, jealousy is as cruel as the grave it brings division among the people of God.

Book of James has the answer, you lust to have something God has given to some one else, you get angry and try and destroy the person to whom the gift belong, you allow the spirit of envy to bring division into the house of God. This spirit is assigned by Satan. The spirit of God cannot work while these spirits are present. These spirits are ministering evil works. Whenever you recognize these spirits, God has commanded you to resist them and pull them down. God expect you to use your gift effectively with appreciation and thanks, you are not to envy the gifts of another. if you ignore your gifts and talents, the day will come as you stand before God, your rewards will be denied.

God has given to you a chance to repent and change your ways. The Holy Spirit will reveal to each Christian the weakness which need deliverance. don't deny the truth, get rid of it. Though the grace the children of God you are forgiven, this is one of the advantage of being spirit filled. the children of Satan does not have the privileged of repentance. God has called us to peace love and unity: the word of God has given us knowledge to know the difference between the good and bad fruit. Gal. 5: 19-23, you shall know them by their fruit. Jealousy brings sorcery, hatred, contention, outburst. The result of jealousy. Saul desired to kill David, Cain killed Abel.

David murdered his lovers husband: this spirit brings murder. It causes abuse between husband and wife and destroys marriages and relationships. Murders are taking place all over the world. Jealousy brings forth wars. This spirit is an enemy of God, Satan uses this weapon against anyone who receive it. when recognized, pull it down. cast it down and destroy it.

love lost In The House Of God

Satan is the fruit of hate
God is the fruit of love

Love has to be constantly taught and demonstrated in the house of God, this subject should not be ignored. Love is a fruit, Gal, 5: 22, and is given to the body of Christ, as a weapon against the enemy, the power of love is stronger than death, it bring peace and salvation to the lost. God so loved the world that he gave his only begotten son to us for salvation, Jesus works are manifested in love, the greatest commandment God gave to his body is to love each other. Without love all is lost, there would be no salvation, no life and no purpose.

Love is nothing until you give it away. The word of God declare in the book of Corinthians 13 Cha. Even thou you speak with tongues and have not love it is useless to God, you may have the gift of prophecy, and understand all mysteries, and all knowledge, you may have all faith to move mountains and have not love God consider it all in vain; you may feed the poor, but if you have love your works are useless.

Love suffers long, love is kind, love envied not, love vaunted not itself, love is not puffed up, love doth not behave it self unseemly, love seek not her own love is not easily provoked, love think no evil, love rejoice not in iniquity but rejoice in the truth, love bear all things, love endure all things. Love never fail, prophecies fail, tongue shall cease. Knowledge it shall vanish away and now abides faith, hope, charity, these three but the greatest of these is love. Jesus is coming for his church, those who has obeyed his commandment of love.

The king loved Ester, he held out the septum which saved her life. David loved Jonathan, Ruth loved her mother-in-law Ruth God loved Jesus, Jesus lover his father Jesus love us, we are commanded to love God and Jesus. You cannot love one without loving the other. Jesus said I and my father are one. Luke 6:35, love your enemies, do good to them that despise you.

Competition in the house of God

Competition comes from Satan; Satan is a phony, and a counterfeit, Satan is constantly trying to compete with God, every thing God does, Satan tries to copy and compete, God has a host of angels, Satan has a host of demons, God's ministers are prophets and prophetess, Satan's ministers are witches and warlock, sorcerers, God's ministers in the old testament, Exodus 7:11, 12, Moses and Aaron under the direction of God threw down their rod it became a serpent: Pharaoh's sorcerers, like manner with their enchantment, threw down their rods. Their rods became serpents. Moses and Aaron's serpents ate up the sorcerers serpents. In the new testament,

God uses his leaders though the Holy Spirit. Satan is yet working evil. He continues to work in magic and witchcraft.

Satan's ministries read palms and do fortune telling God's ministers work miracles though the anointing: Satan performs miracles using demonic powers. Satan has set his ministers among the body of Christ, these demonic spirits posing as ministers of God. Satan even tries to compete with the God Head, the father, son and the Holy Ghost: during the time of the antichrist, Satan will have a false prophet, a beast and an image: those who are left here during the tribulation will bow down and worship the image of the beast which is Satan.

Competition is a spirit sent from Satan, and is being demonstrated in the house of God and has brought God's people under bondage. The spirit of competition is one of Satan's powerful weapon. Whenever you recognize this spirit you are to resist it and pull it down 2,Cor.10:4. Keep out of the lane of the other person's gift, work in your lane and your purpose, if you do this, this spirit will flee. The spirit of competition is in action, it has ministers competing against one another; church members are competing, Job workers are competing: God has made each person unique with unique gifts; he has given individually their own ministry and purpose differs from another. God will allow you to succeed in that which you are called to do. otherwise you will fail. don't get angry with a person because of their accomplishments: The word of God said rejoice with those who rejoice.

SPIRITUAL GIFT FOR THE WORK OF THE MINISTRY

God has commanded us to edify the body of Christ using our gifts and talents. God has ordained, predestinated, commanded and anointed you for the job and has trusted them into your hands. God has given many gifts to the body of Christ which operate in different areas of ministry, but all operate by the same spirit, the word of God expresses, if every one is doing the same ministry, the body would suffer need, every gift is needed within the body of Christ and serves it's purpose in the work of God.

When making a cake a variety of ingredient are needed to bake the cake, if any of the ingredient are missing the cake will fail it's completeness. and if one members suffer all the members suffer with it, or if one member is honored, 1 Corinthians Cha.12. Roman 12:4 We have many members in one body but all the members do not have the same function. If one member is honored all the members are to rejoice with it, there should be no Jealousy.

One body, unity and the diversity

1Corinthians 12: 1 now concerning spiritual gifts I will not have you ignorant. 1 Corinthians 12:14-25 enlightens your eyes to the need of the body concerning the spiritual gifts, verse 23, the members of the body which we think to be less honorable, upon these we bestow more abundant honor, and our uncomely parts have more abundantly comeliness, verse 25, that shall be no schism in the body, but that member should have the same care one for another, if we follow God's principles competition will be eliminated from the house of God. while men slept the enemy crept

33

in,(the church slept) the tares and Satan's ministers came in, Jesus said, I know they are there, when I come I will separate.

Preparation And Assignments

Jesus assigned his disciples and prepared them for spiritual warfare against the powers of darkness; Matthew, Mark. Luke, John, James, Peter, Judas. They walked and talked with him, he taught his disciples the words which his father spoken to him. they are witnesses of miracles Jesus preformed: We all must go though the preparation season. Success in ministry is being an effective soul winner, other wise your ministry is a failure. Effectiveness can only be achieved though the Holy Spirit.

Leadership and preparation

Preparation for leadership causes God's leaders to be effective in their divine purpose.

Wilderness experiences

The wilderness experience is a dry and lonely place of hard test and trials, every leader and child God must have a wilderness experience: one of the most important test in the wilderness is humility, we all must humble our selves before the hands of the almighty God. Each child of God has their personal test in the wilderness. Jesus was led into the wilderness forty days to be tempted of the devil, he defeated Satan with the word of God. The Holy Spirit is the main attraction and the teacher in the wilderness, he teaches us to depend on him as our source. Your motivation in the wilderness should consist of prayer.

God plan is to strip us of all wisdom and worldly ways which we have learned. You have a choice in the wilderness either to stay and conquer or retreat and fail the test. In the wilderness your motivation will be consistent of prayer. Moses was a wilderness example, he was in God's preparation class for forty years, his assignment from God was to deliver the children of Israel from slavery out of the hands of the Egyptians. before God could use

Moses he had to strip him from everything he has learned from pharaoh and the Egyptians. God prepared him before he sent to out.

David's wilderness experience was out in the field shepherd to the sheep, his impossible task was slaying the lion and the bear, which prepared him for his great task of slaying the giant: David was being prepared for his destiny as king of Israel. You may have a back seat now, but faithfulness to God, moves you up.

A medical general practitioner must have at least eight years of university training. Would you put your life in the hands of a medical doctor who had no medical education? Or had a few months of training? Spiritual Warriors are spiritual Doctors, they must be trained for the work of delivering souls and bringing them into the kingdom of God, which requires special training each person has their own personal experience in the wilderness, your best friend

Your husband your wife, your children. Your mother, your father your family, your pastor are not invited: this road you must travel alone. You cannot sneak them in, you can not pray them in, you can bribe them in, your wilderness appointment is designed only for you.

He Who Win A Soul I Wise

Jesus was moved with compassion when he saw the multitude, they are like sheep having no shepherd, pray the Lord send laborers into the harvest, Matt.9

The bible states, he who win a soul is wise, wisdom comes from God. after the souls are bought into the church, the souls has to be lead into the water baptism and then brought into the deliver room, the soul will travail as a woman giving birth paining to be delivered as the Holy Spirit is presented to them: the Holy Spirit will come forth with a voice of power and freedom, the Holy Spirit will speak with an unknown language though the individual. the tongues indicate the person has received the gift of the Holy Ghost.

The evidence has been presented and now the new birth has been completed. After the deliverance has been performed, the soul has to be taught to eat and digest God's spiritual food which is the word of God. If the word of God is properly ministered, the new converts will be guided into the transformed from being transformed from the fleshly Man to the spiritual man. Souls are valuable to heaven. souls depends on your training in the school of the Holy Spirit which is taught by the holy spirit. The spirit teaches the deep things of God, 1 John 2:27.

Jesus said to Simon, launch out your net into the deep and let it down Simon said, we have toiled all night and have caught nothing, nevertheless at your word, I will let down the net, And when they has done this, they caught a great number of fish, and their net was breaking. Jesus said, follow me and I will make you fishers of men, Mat.4:19. Obedience is better than sacrifice. God has chosen us into his ministry, he expect us to work his ministry according to his rules. God's word said, there is a way seem right but it lead to destruction:the right Is God's way.

God is not coming back for the crowd, but for a people who has made them selves ready for his coming. He is coming back for his spirit which is the Holy Spirit and his fruit which is the fruit of the spirit, Galatians Cha. 5:22. Jesus is coming back for his spirit the Holy Spirit. You body, your clothes, your material Possessions none of these things are welcome, they all will remain here on this earth. Since we are made in the image of God, the bible say we shall be like him, he is a spirit. We shall be a spirits and We shall see him as he is.

Preparation In The Potters House

Preparation for the effective work, we must all take a trip to the potters house. Jeremiah 18:2-6, arise and go down to the potter's house, and there I will cause you to hear my words. Then I went down to the potter's house, and behold, he wrought a work on the wheel and the vessel that was made of clay was marred in the hands of the potter: so he made it again another vessel, as seem good for the potter to make it then the word of the Lord came unto me saying, O house of Israel, cannot I do with you as this potter? Says the Lord, as the clay is in the potter's hand, so you are in my hands, O house of Israel: nevertheless the foundation stands sure having this seal the Lord know them that are his. Let everyone who name the name of Christ depart from iniquity.

But in a great house there are not only vessels of gold and silver, but also of wood and of earth, and some of honor and some of dishonor, 2 Timothy 9:20-21. If a man also purge himself from these, he shall be a vessel unto honor, sanctified and meet the master's use, prepared unto every good work. Flee from youthful lust, follow righteousness, faith, charity, peace, with them that call on the name of the Lord with a pure heart. but now o Lord, thy are our father, we are the clay and thy are the potter :We are in thy hands, Isaiah 64:8.

The vessels God has chosen of honor are those he chosen in John 15:16, you did not choose me I chose you and appointed you, that you should go and and bear fruit, and your fruit should remain; God causes you to bear fruit and then he prunes you, John 15:2, that you bear more fruit, he then take you to the potter's house he work continually on his chosen vessel until we are stripped of things that are not useful to the kingdom. You are commanded to study God's word, Timothy 2: 15. which prepares you for the testing. So at your time of testing you will defeat Satan. You will be cast into the fiery furnace, the heat will be turned up seven times hotter: if you are not prepared you will lose the battle. During our school days, first, we were taught, second, we studied, third, time for testing: passing the test depends on you paying attention to the lesson, otherwise you will flunk the test. no test. no testimony. Daniel 3:19, Shadrach, Meshach and Abednego, was prepared for the test, they passed the test and came out victorious.

God Prunes His Vessels of Honor

Prune is to cut off dead or unwanted parts of branches, John 15:2, we are the branches, God cut off or remove everything that is not useful to his kingdom

John 15: 2, Every branch in me that bear fruit, he purges it, cleanse and purify it, that it may bring forth more fruit. Your destiny is determined by God, and has been designed for God's glory: pruning and purging brings us into spiritual maturity.

We are the grapes, God is the grape trader, he crushes us, the crushing is hard and painful, but God will never cruse our spirits, the crushing is not to make us bitter but to make us better. The crushing brings new and fresh wine of his spirit to flow though us, his anointing.

We are not to resist the crushing but to welcome it, the crushing yields much fruit, John 15:2. Every chosen child of God must go though the grape vine. Before God can get glory out of your life you must be pruned and purged.

God Enlisted You Into His Army

All solders are commanded to work with Christ, 2 Cor,6:1, we are workers together with Christ. before you were placed in your mother's womb, God enlisted you into his army 2Timithy 2:4 no soldier in active service entangles himself in the affairs of the everyday life, so he may please him who chose him to be a soldier.

Roman 8: 30, moreover whom he did predestinate, them he also called and whom he called, them he also justified, and whom he justified he also glorified. You are sealed until the day of redemption, what shall we say then if God be for us who can be against us? Who shall separate us from the love of God? Shall tribulation, (no), distress (no), persecution (no), famine (no) shall nakedness {no} peril (no), or sword (no). nay in all things we are more than conquerors though him that loved us. for I am persuaded that neither death nor life nor angels nor principalities nor powers nor things present, nor things to come nor height, nor depth, nor any other creature, shall be able to separate us from the love of God, which is in Christ Jesus Our Lord.

A Chosen Warrior

A chosen warrior cannot be conquered, broken, stopped nor defeated, he or she expands in the mist of contraction, a chosen warrior is determined and persistence, a chosen warrior faces the enemy and go into combat when necessary, a chosen warrior is aware of their spiritual nature, constantly getting renewal of mind, a true warrior refuses to entangle his or herself again with the yoke of bondage, a chosen warriors fights a good fight of faith, a chosen warrior always aims for victory, a true warrior submits to the holy spirit, a true warrior is constantly moving into maturity A true warrior follows instructions of the master.

God expect his warriors to grow in the army rank. You do not start out as a general in God's army, you are private first, working in booth camp, you must discipline your flesh and submit to God and the holy spirit. Gal. 5:22. As you grow and submit to God, he will move you to new levels in his army: your promotion comes with maturity as God moves you into higher ranks

Chosen generation

God is raising up a generation who has the heart of God such as David Joshua, Esters, Ruth, Deborah and many others of the chosen generation.

David—heart of repentance
Joshua—faith, strength and courage
Ester—dedicated, courage, faith, faithful
Deborah—a prophetess, warrior, strong. Courage, wise, faithful
Ruth—faithful, loyal.

1 Peter 2: 9, but you are a chosen generation, a royal priesthood an holy nation, a peculiar people, that ye should show forth the praise of him who hath called you out of darkness into the marvelous light, God is raising up in this season a generation who will obey, leaders who will rule over his people with love and sincerity, The word of God says when the righteous rule the people rejoice. Ps.9:2, I will be glad and rejoice in it.

Downfall Of Old Testament Leaders

We have leaders in the old testament who disobeyed God, such as Saul, God brought judgment on Saul and replaced him with David. We are warriors called for battle we cannot allow ourselves to become carnal, carnality causes us to become an enemy to God. as warriors of God, you must train your ears to hear the spirit of God. In spiritual warfare you must follow God's instructions to win the battle. relationship with God bring you into the present of the spirit and gives you access to enter in behind the veil.

Sampson+ disobedience

was a warrior and a conqueror, a man God chosen to fight and defeat the philistines, the philistines were enemies of the children of Israel, God anointed Sampson with the strength in his hair, and commanded him not to cut it. This mighty man of God allowed his flesh to interfere with his divine assignment, he was deceived by a woman, she deceived him and sold him to the enemy, the enemy came upon him cut his hair robbed him of his strength, he was captured and taken into slavery, he lost his power and became helpless against his enemy. This powerful man allowed himself to become side tracked during the time of battle, he took off his amour, and laid down his weapons. Sampson's downfall should be a lesson to all who are chosen for battle. stay focus on your assignment, never take off your amour nor should you lay down your weapons: your spiritual life depends on your spiritual dress code. Obedience is better than sacrifice.

Saul+ disobedience

Saul was chosen by God as king over Israel. He was commanded by God never to seek after one who had an familiar spirit, he disobeyed, 1Samuel 15: 16, the spirit of the Lord departed from Saul: 1 Samuel 28:7, he sought after a woman who had a familiar spirit and enquired of her, to speak to Samuel who were dead, he paid the price with his life, he and his sons were killed. Obey God.

David + disobedience

David had Uriah killed and married his wife. He fell into disobedient, God said The sword shall never depart from your house because you have despises me and have taken the wife of Uriah to be your wife: David was spared from God's wrath because he had a heart of repentance, Ps 51, he cried out to God and God forgave him. obedience is better than sacrifice. If you fall into sin do not remain in it get up and repent.

The Chosen

Matthew 22: 14, many are called but few are chosen

John15:16 You have not choose me but I chosen you and ordained you.

You are chosen and equipped for battle

John 17:14 Jesus said, I have given them thy word and the world has hated them because they are not of this world even as I am not of this world verse

19, I have given them thy word, verse 17, Sanctify them through thy truth. John,17:17, as Thy hast sent me into the world even so I sent them into the world. Our steps has been ordered by the Lord, we are instructed by Jesus to go into battle. Warriors it's time to go, work while it is day, when night come your time is up, the clock is ticking, tomorrow is not promised, your life can be gone tomorrow.

Ask your self a question? {What has God called me to do} pass out tracks, be a witness, preach, teach, intercessory prayer, lay hands on the sick, cast out demons or sing in the choir, what ever God has called you to do obey the call, if you are of age, the bible say let the older woman teach the younger woman, Pray for the saints, pray for the leaders, Pray for the youth, pray for souls, pray for backsliders. you are assigned to work, God has given you a Job here on this earth to dominate the powers of darkness.

Every time you use your God given gifts and talents you are dominating the power of Satan. We are equipped with power Act 1: 8. Though the Holy Spirit, Matt 10:1, Jesus called his twelve disciples he gave them power against unclean spirits, to cast them out, and to heal all matters of sick diseases. Jesus has given you the same power and authority. don't be afraid to use it. Jesus said it is not robbery to be equal with God, which mean, you are equal in power, he's in you.

Habakkuk 3: 19, the Lord is my strength and he will make my feet like hind feet and he will make me to walk upon my high places: high places in the anointing. Christ is the anointed one, he and his father has made their abode in us, the father the son and the Holy Ghost, all three are one and are in us, Jesus said, when you see me you see the father I and my father are one. Whenever you face the enemy In battle, God's light in you blinds your enemies and it run them off.

God Allegiance Transferred From Adam To Satan

Because of Adam's sin, God allegiance was transferred from Adam to Satan, he became god of this world. Because of Satan being god of this world, **he had** claim on humanity and slain millions because at that time **he had** the power to exercised it upon others. **He was** a slave owner, and had legal title to all offspring of his slave, Satan had legal title of Adam sons and could do with them what he wished. God has a divine law, under God's divine law pronounced

Satan a murderer of a innocent victim upon whom he had no claim, **he had no claim on Jesus** because Jesus knew no sin. Therefore Satan became subject in the court of universal Justice, to the death penalty. Satan brought upon himself the penalty of death, he destroyed Himself, Hebrew 2:14, forasmuch then as the children are partakers of the flesh and blood, he also himself likewise took part of the same. that though death he might destroy him that had the power of death, that is the devil.

God Allegiance Transferred From Satan To Jesus

We are delivered from the powers of Satan at Calvary though the blood of Jesus. all his legal claims has been cancelled. Satan has absolutely no right at all upon anyone or anything. Which mean the power which he exercises now he exercises by deception and bluff. Jesus said, Matt, 28:18, All power is given to me in heaven and in earth. In Luke 10:19, Jesus uses his authority and said, Behold which mean {see}, I give unto you power to tread on serpents and scorpions {demons} and over all the power of the enemy, and nothing shall hurt you.

Because Jesus knew no sin, according to God's divine law. Satan slew an innocent man: God sent Jesus and Jesus sent us and commanded that we build the kingdom of God. **Though the death of Jesus, Satan was defeated in the conflict.** The death of Jesus destroyed Satan, **all of Satan claims has been cancelled upon the earth and the human race.** According to God's divine law Satan was a murderer of an innocent victim upon he had no claim and became subject in the court of universal justice: Jesus said I free give my life.

I lay down my life for the sheep, John 10: 15. God sent Jesus, Jesus has sent us to build the kingdom on earth, to bind evil on the earth and loose good in heaven, bringing thy kingdom on earth as it is in heaven. we are preparing the earth for the coming of the Lord. The victory was won on Calvary, but there are laws has to be enforced.

The president won the election but there are law has to be enforced. Calvary's victory was placed in the hands of the church, Christ corporate a body upon the earth, the body with hands and feet is the vehicle carries out the command of the head, If the body fail to respond, the will of the head become a dead letter, the authority to enforce Christ's victory over Satan was delegated to the church in Matthew16:18.

We enforce God law when we walk as a lights in a dying world and preach his word without compromise, to a sinful nation and proving ourselves genuine Christians. Loving, giving and caring, reaching out to all who are in despair.

Christ took the keys from Satan

After Jesus died on the cross, he went to hell, took the keys of death and the hell from the devil and said, I am he who live forever and was dead, behold I am alive forever, I have the keys to death and the grave, the door way of hell was unhinged at the name of Jesus, hell was a place of agony, his soul suffered, he suffered in our stead, he suffered until the mind of God, the eternal justice was met, Christ conflict and trump in the infernal region, when the claim of eternal justice was fully discharged, Christ was justified in the spirit.

1Peter 3: 18, our spirit was completely cut off and separated from God in order to be made alive unto God and restored to fellowship, Jesus had to die on the cross: when Christ was exalted the church was enthroned, when Christ took his seat in heaven proved that Satan's devastation was thrown into bankruptcy, stripped of his legal authority and dominion and stripped of his weapons. Jesus has given us the keys of the kingdom and the authority to use them, we are citizens of the kingdom, we have been given the keys to our new home.

We have the power to bind and to loose: whatever we bind on earth effects heaven, whatsoever we loose on earth effects heaven so, whatsoever we close on earth heaven closes. Whatsoever we loose on earth heaven looses. For God is the kingdom, the power and the glory forever amen. The power is in the keys. Jesus took the keys from Satan and gave them to his chosen. We are in control of keys to your house, if you give someone the keys to your door, your attitude is saying You trust the individual, you will not give your keys to an enemy, but to a Trust worthy friend. Jesus has given the keys to those whom he can trust.

WE ARE SEATED IN HEAVENLY PLACES WITH CHRIST

When Jesus busted forth from that dark prison and ascended upon high, all believers were raised and seated together with Christ, but only those who believe are identified with him in his resurrection and exaltation and enthronement. God said, he that is joined unto the Lord is one spirit:

1 COR. 6:17, things has been legally put under Jesus feet. Jesus snacked the keys of death and the grave from Satan and busted forth from abyss, we were sharer in the trump, when he ascended up on high and took his seat in the heaven, we were exalted with him, Satan's dominion ended at Calvary, we are seated in heavenly places with Christ. Satan realize we are his master, he bluffs the church in deception. Satan know he has lost the battle, the best he can do is harass and sabot you. Satan sends his demons to tire you out by persistent effort of attacks, to worry and annoy you, God has given us the victory. You are commanded to walk in victory. We are ordained to win, losing is not an option.

God builds his church on his word

I say unto thee, thou are Peter and upon this rock I will build my church and the gates of hell shall not prevail against it. Whosoever hear these saying of mine, and does them, he is a wise man who build his house on the rock, and the trouble came, the rain, the floods and the wind came and beat on that house and it did not fall because it was strong on the rock, Ephesians 7: 24+25. Be strengthen in the Inner man, being rooted and grounded in the word, Ephesians 3:16+17.

God has chosen us as agents of enforcement of Calvary's victory to stand on the word. God word is settled in heaven and cannot be altered, he said let God be the truth and every man a lie. Adam's disobedient did not stop the plan of God. Ephesians 1:5, God has chosen us in him before the foundation of the world.

Worker Together With Christ

Working with Christ is being in agreement with the word of God Ephesians 2:10, we are his workmanship, he has given to us the character, quality and the skills to get the job done as workers together with Christ and working together with each other in peace, 2 Corinthians 6:1. Ephesians 4:31, be kind hearted toward one another. Philippians 4:3 Paul said, I entreat thee also, **true yokefellow, help those women which labor with me In the gospel, whose names are written in the book of life**. Preachers, Pastors ask the Holy Spirit to show you the chosen woman of God and help Them to do the will of God expect you to have the right mind set, not for selfish purposes, but in obedience to God, realizing one day you will stand before God and be Judge for your motives, God will hold you accountable, because you were a hinder to the work of God. Be true to your self and be true to God.

God said know them who labor among you. His commandment is have no prospect of person; disobedient will cause the body to suffer. Ephesians 2: 19-21, we are fellow citizen with the saints, and of the house of the corner stone, if You desire to build upon the foundation of the apostles and the prophets and Jesus you must build your foundation on the rock: Matthew,7:24-27: Jesus said upon this rock I shall build my church and the very gates of hell shall not prevail against it. The word of God is the rock. Gal. 1: 8-10, but though we, are an angle from heaven, preach any other gospel unto you than that which we have preached unto you, let him be accursed.

BELIEVERS ARE HEALED

God's word clearly states you are healed by his stripes, God is not a God to lie, believe and receive your healing. One of the most powerful weapons God has given you to use against your opponent is faith, Faith destroys all powers of Satan. this shield is a spiritual light, demons are terrified of light. the shield of faith quenches the fiery darts of Satan's kingdom {quench} put out the devil's fire, stops him and defeats his power.

God's word cannot be altered, Isaiah 53: 5, and with his stripes we are healed, believe it. You are healed from every sickness and disease. Psalm 107: 20, Jesus sent his word and healed them. Matthew 4:23, Jesus went about healing all matter of sickness and disease. They bought unto him all the sick, the diseased and those who had torments and healed them. They believed and were healed.

Matthew 8:5-10, a centurion, beseeched Jesus in the behalf of his servant lie at home sick of the palsy, Jesus said I will come and heal him, the centurion said, I am not worthy that you should come under my roof but speak the word, and my servant shall be healed. The centurion believed and received his miracle, Jesus marveled at his faith and said go thy way, as thy has believed, so be unto you. his servant was healed in that same hour, the moment the centurion spoke the word and believed it, his servant was healed.

Speak the word of healing for your sickness believe it and receive it, the manifestations of your healing shall spring forth. {[**Manifest**} to show plainly, make evident, display, evidence of the things unseen. Something is present but not yet seen. Faith brings in the manifestation.

Pearl Davis

{**Manifestation**} the act, process, a public demonstration of power and purpose, Matthew 12:22, demons were cast out, the blind and the dumb both spoke and their eyes were opened because of there belief. Luke 8: 43-48, the woman who had the issue of blood for twelve years and spent all her money to doctors for years she lacked faith, her faith was in the wrong place, the moment she believed and spoke the word of faith, at that same hour she was healed. Sickness is not from God, Satan is the author of sickness and falls under spiritual wickedness. Resist sickness it will flee.

Sickness can come from bitterness, unforgiveness, hatred, Jealousy, envy and fear. If you are weak in these areas do not deny it, Face your fears, find scripture for each one, pray and fast and cast them down.

Cancer, tumors, sugar diabetes, blood pressure, blood disease, stomach problems, eye disease, ear disease, kidney problem: faith destroys every sickness Satan has Assigned to you; believe God, nothing is too hard for God to do. His word, believe I am able to do exceedingly abundantly and above all you can ask or think, believe he is able to do, he will do it. Cancer has to bow it's knee to Jesus, tumors has to its knee to Jesus, blood pressure has to bow it's knee to Jesus, blood disease has to bow it's knee to Jesus. Stomach problems has to bow it's knee to Jesus, hepatitis has to bow it's knee to Jesus. Kidney problems has to bow his knee to Jesus, heart disease has to bow it's knee to Jesus, sinus has to bow it's knee to Jesus, mind disease has to bow it's knee to Jesus, Lung problems has to bow it's knew to Jesus. Prostate cancer has to bow it's knee to Jesus.

48

FIVE FORE MINISTRIES

The function of the five fore ministry: to trained the sheep and the body of Christ how to function in their gifts and talents and to edify the body of Christ. Jesus said to Peter if thou love me feed my sheep John 21:17. I believe God's sheep are more important to God than his leaders. God is very protective of his sheep and get angry when they are mistreated and mislead:

{Five fore ministry} Ephesians 4:11-15, and he has given some, apostles and some prophets and some, evangelists and some pastors and teachers for the perfecting of the saints, for the work of the ministry, for the edifying of the body of Christ that the people of God be no more tossed to and fro and carried about with every wind of doctrine whom by the sleight of men and cunning craftiness, whereby they lie in wait to deceive the sheep: the five fore ministries are to edify the body of Christ, (building them up) and perfect them in the ways of God.

All believers are chosen for purpose

God has given all believers a purpose and destiny to fulfill. Ephesians 1:4+5, according to as he hath chosen us in him before the foundation of the world, that we should be holy without blame before him in love, having predestinated us unto the adoption of children by Jesus Christ unto himself, according to the good pleasure of his will, to the praise of the glory of his grace, wherein he hath made us acceptable in the beloved. God has given a believer a firm belief in his word. A saint is one who is sanctified in obedient to God in living a holy life.

All believer must seek God for their personal purpose in life. Every believer has purpose in common, which is a witness for Christ, but you shall receive power after the Holy Spirit has come upon you and you shall be witnesses to me. God has given every believer the purpose of bearing fruit, Jesus has chosen and appointed you that you should go and bear fruit, John 15: 16. You are to bring forth the fruit of the spirit, love, joy, peace, longsuffering, kindness, goodness, faithfulness, gentleness and self control, and that your fruit remain. Therefore by him let us continually offering to him the sacrifice fruit of praise, Hebrew 13:15.

Men 0ne of your chosen purpose is your wife

To love cherish and nourishes her. Ephesians 5:25-29, husbands love your wives as Christ loved the church, so husbands ought to love their own wives as their own bodies. Men if you do not give us our need as God has commanded you. You are walking in disobedience. We as woman all are in need of love and affection. Some woman are chosen for ministry, but that does not stop the need for love and affection, because of the fact she is a chosen she need your love even more. God has chosen you as her head to protect and care for her, not to control her or man handle her, but To love, show affection, nourishes and cherish. If you both are in ministry support each other, if not then the one support the other.

God chose a wise man he could trust with Deborah's destiny. God loved her though her husband and provided her with love, affection and nourishment.

I can only speak as a woman, I fill a man is not whole nor does he function properly alone without his help meet, the reason, because God said he need a helpmeet. If he say he is doing find, without her, he is a lie, because God said it is not good for man to be alone, God know a single man will commit fornication. So God's plan for man is marriage: men pastors should teach men the importance of marriage. I believe this subject should be taught by men Pastors. They should also teach them to seek God for their soul mate by fasting and praying.

Woman one of your chosen purpose is your husband

God say you are his help meet, if you are not chosen for ministry, your husband is your ministry and you are to care for your family. If you are chosen for ministry and is married, you are a wife and have duties to perform as a wife, a wise woman know how to separate her ministry and time for her husband, God said, be wise in all things. you are held responsible to God if you do not obey God as your duty as his help meet. God has chosen him as your head, not to control you or man handle you but respect you love and to cherries you. If you are chosen for ministry and desire a husband you must wait on God, for the man of his choice for you. If you both are in ministry support each other.

All married woman weather you are in ministry are not, you are to encourage your husband and build him up. And to do him good all the days of his life. God chose Sarah for Abraham, her ministry was her husband, she called him Lord, she believed in him and supported him in the things of God, she knew he was a man of God. Proverb 31, Who can find a virtuous woman? For her rubies is far above rubies, the heart of her husband safety trust her, so he will have no lack of gain.

She does him good and not evil all the days of her life. She brings her food from afar, she's a praying woman, she rises while it is yet night. Praying during the night. Strength an honor are her clothing, she shall rejoice in the time to come,

She is a woman of wisdom, she opens her mouth with wisdom. And her tongue is the of kindness, her children rise up and call her blessed, her husband also, and He praises her. Many daughters have done well, but you excel them all but she a woman who fears the Lord, she shall be praised. Give her the fruit of her hands, and let her own works praise her in the gates.

Believers are commanded to marry only believers. and be not unequally yoked with unbeliever, if we obey this commandment we walk together in agree. God said, it is impossible for light and darkness to walk together.

God said it is not good for man to be alone

I agree with God's word it is not good to be alone so why are so many of us alone. The reason, Satan hate marriage because marriage represents Christ and it brings unity and strength between the two. Satan work hard at keeping the rightful mates apart, he is aware of the fact that together his kingdom is defeated. We are not ignored of Satan wicked devices So I am asking the body of Christ to pray for the loosing of the rightful mates to come together in marriage within the body of Christ.

God showed me as a prophet—that Satan has attacked the male and female with a spirit of insecurity, doubt and fear, this spirit has been sent to abode the complete marriage system of God: I'm asking the truth church which is the body of Christ to go before God in fasting and praying for God to loose the spirit of marriage within the body of Christ. The word of God said some come out only by fasting and praying. Prayer is a spiritual weapon. We bind insecurity spirits, doubting spirits, fearful spirits and all interfering spirits in the name of Jesus, we bind you on earth, we loose the spirit of marriage in Jesus name.

When the enemy desired to destroy the Jews, Ester called a fast. The people cooperated and the yokes of the enemy was destroyed, and the Jews were saved, Ester was brought to the kingdom at such a time as this.

God has brought us to the kingdom at such a time as this to do battle with our enemies, destroy the powers of darkness, pull down the strong hold of the enemy and loose the blessings to the people of God, we have the power, we are touching and agreeing with the word.

Recover all

Saints let's come together in agreement to recover all Satan has stolen from you together we will recover all, we all know this prayer, if my people who are called by my name humble themselves and pray and turn from their evil ways then God will hear our prayer and heal our land, we come together in prayer and agreement we recover in Jesus name, God said his ears are opened to the righteous and he hear our cry, together we Stand, divided we fall, together we can accomplished anything. We all together will pray this prayer.

Hezekiah's prayer, Cha. 19:19, O God save us from the Assyria's hand that all the kingdoms of the earth may know that you are the Lord God alone: we will pray for God to deliver and save us from our enemies, and deliver the people of God, families, sinners, and every thing he has promised his people, give us the strength to recover all.

GOD'S ANGLES
ARE WORKING FOR US

God has given his angles charge over us. Ps 91:11. We have the authority given to us by God to order angles to help us, they are ministering angles to minister to us and for us. The angels are pure endowed with a natural intelligence, will power and beauty, far surpassing the nature, faculties and power of man. Millions of angels praises and worships God, they serves him as messengers and is guardians of men on earth. They are divided into three hierarchies Seraphim, Cherubim and Thrones Dominations, Principalities and powers, virtues, archangels angles.

PS:91 Each individual has a guardian angels who watches over him during the whole course of his life. The guardian angels defends those of whom they have charge against the assaults of the demons. endeavor to preserve them from all evil of soul or body, Particularly from sin and the occasions of sin. they endeavor to keep us in the right path if we fall, they help us to rise again, they encourage us to become more virtuous that suggest good thoughts and holy desires they offer our prayer and good actions to God, and above all they assist us at the hour of death.

Angle Gabriel was sent from God to a virgin Mary. Luke 1:26, and said, hail thy are highly favored, the Lord is with thee; blessed are thy among woman, thy shall conceive in thy womb, and bring forth a Son, and shall call his name Jesus, the Holy Ghost shall come upon thee, and the power of the highest shall over shadow thee, that holy thing which is born of thee shall be called the son of God.

Geneses 18: 2, three angles appeared to Abraham, angle said, I will return unto thee according to The time of life, thy wife shall have a son at the appointed time.

The angle of the Lord found Hagar by the fountain of water in the wilderness after she has fled from her mistress Sarah. God would not allow Isaac to marry a wife of the Canaanites, but go to his county, and to his kindred and chose a wife for Isaac, Gen 24:7. God sent his angles before Abraham's servant.

The angle of the Lord went before the camp of the Lord of Israel. The angle removed and went behind them and the pillar of cloud went from before their face, and stood behind them, verse 20, And it came between the camp of the Egyptians and the camp of the Israel and it was a cloud and darkness to the Egyptians, but it gave light by night to Israel so that the one came not near the other all night.

An angle touched Elijah, and said, arise and eat a bake cake on the coal and a cruse of water at his head, he ate and drank, this is the time Elijah ran for his life, he received a message Jezebel plan to kill him.

1 king Cha. 19, the angle of the Lord by night opened the prison doors and brought the apostle forth and said, go stand and speak in the temple to the people all the words of life:

blessed be the God of Shadrach, Meshach, and Abednego, who hath sent his angle, and delivered his servants that trust in him, and have changed the king's word and yielded their bodies that they might not serve nor worship any god except their own God.

Daniel said, my God has sent his angle and has shut the lion's mouth and they have not hurt me, God sent angles to destroy of Sodom and Gomorrah grievous because of sin, Two angles came to Sodom, Lot saw them and rose to meet them, and he bowed Himself with his face toward the grown, lot invited them into his house with hospitality, the men of Sodom and Gomorrah said bring them out to us so we may know them, the evil men tried to break down the door, they pulled in lot and Shut the door. The angles smote the men with blindness so they were not able to open the door, the angles said to Lot go and take your family and all your goods and go. for we will destroy this place, because the cry of them has Waxed great before The face of the Lord, and the Lord has sent us to destroy it. The angle said to get out of this city you and your family lest you be consumed. Then the Lord rained upon Sodom and Gomorrah Brimstones and fire from the Lord out of heaven: But his wife looked back and was turned into a pillar of salt.

Daniel Cha. 10: 12+13, a demon in the heaven tried to hinder his answer but Michel God's warrior angle, fought the demon and released the answer

Matt, 24: 29, Immediately after the tribulation of those days shall the sun be darkened, and the moon shall not give her light, and the stars shall fall from heaven, and the power the heaven shall be shaken. The angel will be involved,

Hebrew 1:11, are they all ministering spirits? sent forth to ministry for them who shall be heirs of salvation, Matt. 25: 31, When the Son of Man shall come in his glory, and all the holy angles with him, then shall he sit upon the throne of his glory.

Pilate said I have the power to release you, Jesus said the only power you have is given to you of my father, Jesus said, I can call legions of angles they would come and deliver me out of your hands. Jesus said no man take my life I freely give it.

11King, 6: 8, The King of Syria warred against Israel, his servants was afraid, Elisa said, fear not for they that be for us is more than they that is against us, Elisa prayed, open your eyes and behold the mountain was full of horses and chariots of fire (angle) round about Elisa. Whenever you are surrounded with demons do no fear, God has assigned angles encamped around you to help you. The chariot of God is twenty thousand and thousands of angles, Psalm 68:17.

God Give Power To His Prophet

JER. 1: 9+ 10, then he touched my mouth, see. Today, I have put my word in your mouth, to warn the nations and the kingdoms of this world, I have given you the power to pluck up, to break down, to destroy and to overthrow to build, to plant to nourish my people and to make them strong and great. The body of Christ are the true church. the church has to grow up and take their place as the sons of God, the world is waiting on you.

Roman 8: 19, for the earnest expectation of the creature waits for the manifestation of the sons of God. Verse 21, because the creature itself also shall be delivered from the bondage of corruption into the glorious liberty of the children. God is waiting for his church to mature to deliver the captive from the powers of darkness. Wake up out of your sleep, get up from your comfort zone stop your foolishness, look at the time, listen to the cry of souls. Work while it is day when your night come on you will not be able to work, old age sickness or even death, what have you done for Christ, have you accomplished your purpose, have you obeyed your call, are you running the race with patience.

GOD SENDS HIS PROPHETS OUT WITH REVELATION

Matt,10:16, Behold I send you as sheep in the midst of wolves be wise as a serpent and humble as a dove. God reveals unto his servants wisdom how to dig deep into his treasures [his word]the revelation] of his riches in secret places, so that the eyes of your understanding being enlightened that you may know what is the hope of his calling, and what the riches of his glory of his inheritance in the saints, Ephesians 1:18.

God said I will give you treasures of darkness and riches in secret places, that you may know that I, the Lord which call thee by thy name, am the God Israel, Isaiah 45: 3. surely the Lord will do nothing, but he reveals his secret unto his servants the prophets, the lion hath roared, who will not fear? The Lord God has spoken, who can but prophesy? Amos 3:7, he revealed the deep and secret things, he know what is in the dark and the light dwells with him, Daniel 2:22. friendship with God is reserved for those who reverence him with them alone he shares the secret of his promises, PS. 25:14.

Old Testament Prophets + Servants

Abraham, Moses, Caleb, Samson, Elijah, Isaiah, Debra, Ester, Ruth Jeremiah, Ezekiel, Daniel, Hosea, Amos, Micah, Zephaniah, Haggai.

God Sends Abraham

Genesis Chapter 12: 1 God's assignment to Abraham was faith, he was to leave his country, his family and his father's house and go to an unfamiliar land, God Promised him as he moved by faith he would show him the land he promised him, Genesis 12: 2. I will make of you a great nation, I will bless thee and the seed. and make thy name great, and thy shall be a blessing and all the families of the earth shall be blessed, (this is a covenant promise to you of faith)Abraham started out on the promises of God at the age of seventy years. God showed him all the land which he promised to give him, I will bless you and your seed, (we are the seed of Abraham.

Abraham believed God, Even before the promise was manifested Abraham faith was strong V-18. he build an alter and worshiped God by faith. Abraham is an example to all believer. We are challenge to worship God in the form of praise and worship him for his promises. every word of God has been accomplished in heaven, it is done. God's promises to Abraham concerning the promise child: The promise came to pass, Gen.17:19. God promised to make Ishmael and Isaac great nations, the promises came to pass. We are part of those promises they too shall come to pass.

God Sends Moses Out

God prepared Moses for his assignment before he sent him out on his mission. Moses killed a Hebrew for smiting an Hebrew; because he feared Pharaoh he fled, Exodus Cha. 2. during the time of his disappearance, God put him in training, after his training was completed, God sent him out on his assignment. Go and deliver my people Israel from the hands of Pharaoh. God showed Moses the revelation and the victory from the beginning to the end of the task, and demonstrated to him his power. Moses accomplished his purpose in victory.

Moses was chosen before the foundation of the world, to deliver the children of Israel from the hand of Pharaoh, the enemy tried to kill him before his mission but God kelp him alive for his purpose.

God Sent Jesus

For God so love the world that he gave his only begotten son that he whoever believe shall have not perish but shall have ever lasting life.

John 10:1, Jesus said I am the good shepherd, as the father know me even though I know the father, and I lay down my life for the sheep there fore my father love me, because I lay down my life That I might take it again, no man take it from me but I lay it down of myself. I have power to lay it down and I have power to take it. No human has the power to lay his life down and pick it up, only God. Jesus said I and my father are one, when you see me you see the father. Jesus is a precious gift, most valuable than any gift on the earth.

Jesus Sent You

John, 17:18, Jesus said, as thou hast sent me into the world, even so have I sent you into the world. you have not chosen me but I have chosen you, John 15: 16. He has sent us as the salt of the earth as world changers. Go and search for the lost, tell them Jesus saves and of his death on the cross for them on the cross for their sin. Tell them if they believe in the son of Jesus Christ, they shall have eternal life, tell them that God gave his only begotten son that whosoever believe in Him shall not perish but shall have ever lasting life, John 14 Cha.

Let them to know they do not have to die in sin, the price had been paid for their freedom. Let them to know their heart need no longer to be trouble. They are to believe in God and also in Jesus, tell them Satan has come to destroy but Jesus came to give them life.

Tell them they must be born again of the water and the Holy Spirit. Tell them Jesus has the power to heal their broken heart and their wounded Spirit. Tell them Jesus can deliver them from drug and alcohol addiction. You are Jesus mouth, hands and feet. You are his instrument.

Pray for them, fast for them, comfort them, love them. If your gift is laying on of hands, lay hands on them and pray for them. Witness to them of your experiences and how God delivered you. Lead them to Christ. Witness to them the power of God, let them to know after they receive the Holy Spirit they too shall have power. Let them know God is a miracle working

God and there is nothing too hard for him to do. Either you believe God or you don't. If you believe him you will obey him. If you are waiting on people to help you. You will be disappointed. When you stand before God he will ask you what did you do with his gifts and talents, how will you answer him, the only answer to please God will be I have run a good race, finished my course and kelp the faith.

SATAN ASSIGNS HIS ANGLES TO PERVERT THE EDUCATION SYSTEM

Satan has planted his angels in the house of God as counterfeit leaders among the wheat, Satan assigned them to the educational system to try and pervert the word of God. The word of God cannot be altered. the counterfeit leaders has caused God's people to err from the truth, they will not spare the sheep nor do they care for their souls. The bible say they judge for reward and the priest teach for hire, his watchman are blind they are all ignorant, they are all dumb dogs Isaiah 56: 10:12. they cannot bark, sleep, lying down loving to slumber: Verse 11, they are greedy dogs, they can never have enough, and they are shepherds that can not understand they all look to their own way every one for gain, from the quarter. Verse 12, come ye say they, I will fetch wine, and we will fill our selves with strong drink, and tomorrow shall be as this day and much more abundant.

Matt, 15:14, let them alone, they be blind leaders and if the blind lead the blind they both fall into the ditch.

Luke 21:8, take heed that you be not deceived, 2 Tim: 3:13, but evil men and impostors will proceed from bad to worse, deceiving and being deceive.

Beware Of Deceivers

Because of the deceivers, Paul wrote, Act 20:29, for I know this, that after my departure shall grievous wolves enter in among you, not sparing the flock. Also of your own selves shall men arise speaking perverse things, to draw away disciples after them.

John Cha 4: 1, Believe not every spirit but try the spirit whether they are of God. because false prophets are gone out into the world Verse5, They are of the world, they speak of the world and the world hear them. We are of God they of God hear us, know the spirit of truth and the spirit of error, Matt 7:16, know the truth and the truth shall make you free, you shall know them by their fruit. 1Titus10, For there are many unruly and vain talkers and deceivers especially they of the circumcisions whose mouths must be stopped, who pervert whole houses, teaching things they ought not, for filthy lucre's sake. Paul said, verse13, This witness is true, wherefore rebuke them sharply, that they may be sound in the faith.

Verse 15, unto the pure all things pure, but unto them that are defiled and unbelieving is nothing pure but even their minds and conscience is defiled, they confess they know God, but in works they deny him, being abominable, and disobedient, and unto every good work reprobate. These are working and building, their mouth speak of him but they are denying God because their hearts are far from him, therefore their works are in vain.

Prophecy of the scripture

2 Peter 1: 20+21Knowing this first, that no prophecy of the scripture is of any private interpretation, for the prophecy came not in old time by the will of men but Holy men of God as they were moved by the Holy Ghost. Timothy 3:16, All scripture is given by inspiration of God, and is profitable for doctrine, for reproof, for correction, for instruction in righteousness. That the man of God be perfect, thoroughly furnished unto good works.

So that you will not be ignorant concerning Satan wicked devices but will have the knowledge of God's word. These men who were moved by the Holy Spirit were obedient submitted and willing. God trusted these men with the most valuable treasure on earth, his word which has set mankind free. God's word is truth and not a lie. Apostle Paul said if any man preach any other gospel except Jesus and him being crucified, which I have preached let him be accursed.

False prophets among the people

2 Peter 2:1-3, But there were false prophets also among the people, even as there shall be false teachers among you, who privately shall bring in damnable heresies, even denying the Lord that bought them, and bring upon themselves swift destruction. Verse 2, and many shall follow their pernicious ways, by reason of whom the truth shall be evil spoken. And though covetousness shall they with feigned words make merchandise of you, whose judgment now, and their damnation slumbered not. They promise you liberty while they themselves are servant corruption, the thing you have overcome, the same you can be brought into bondages, the only way out of bondage is true heart of repentance.

2 Peter, 2:18, do not be allure in by their charm and attraction, after they have allured you in, you become entangle in a yoke of bondage. know the truth and the truth shall make you free, John 8: 32. 2 Peter 2: 9, The Lord know how to deliver the Godly out of temptation, and to reserve the unjust unto the day of judgment to be punished. nevertheless the foundation of God stands sure having this seal the Lord know them that are his, Let every one that name the name of Christ depart from iniquity, 2 Timothy 2:19.

Verse 13, hold fast the form of sound word. Cha 2: 2, and the things which you have heard of me, commit to faithful men, who shall be able to teach others also. Verse 15, study to show yourself approved unto God a workman that needed not to be ashamed, rightly dividing the word of truth. the preacher cannot stand before God for you, on that day you have an appointment to stand before God for you self.

Paul words, 1 Corinthians 2: 4, my speech and my preaching was not with enticing words of man's wisdom. But in demonstration of the spirit and the power of God. Having a degree is find, but God is looking for those who are obedient and are willing to follow the direction of the Holy Spirit, those who has been shaped and fired to be formed Into Godly leaders and Salvation Ministers.

Roman 6: 23, the wedges of sin is death but the gift of God is eternal life: Roman 5:6, what shall we say then shall we continue in sin that grace may abide ? God forbid: even though God has grace for the believers but one day the saints will also stand before God for the evil thoughts and actions toward their brother: 2 Peter 3:1 second epistle, beloved, I now write unto you in both which I stir up your pure minds by way of remembrance that you be mindful of the words which were spoken before by the Holy prophets and of the commandment of us.

The True Prophet
Expose The False Prophets

Jeremiah 22: 2 Woe! unto the Pastors that destroys and scatters the sheep of my Pastures said the Lord, therefore thus said he Lord of Israel, I am against the Pastors that feed my people, you have scattered my flock, and driven them away and have not visit them, behold, I will visit upon you the evil of your doing, said the Lord, commit adultery and walk in lies, they strengthen the wicked, they are all unto me as Sodom and Gomorrah. Jeremiah 23:16 thus said the Lord of host harkens not unto the words of the prophets that prophesy unto you, they make you vain, they speak a vision of their own heart and not from the mouth of God they say the lord has said, you shall have peace and they say unto every one that walk after the imagination of their own heart no evil shall come upon you; they speak lies to the people, 23: 21 I have not sent these prophets yet they ran:

Verse 23:28 saying I have dreamed, How long shall this be in the heart of the prophets that prophesy lies? Yea, they are prophets of deceit of their own heart which cause my people to forget my name, this prophet that has a dream tell it as a dream and he that has my word let him speak my word faithfully, verse 29 what is the chaff to the wheat? Said the Lord light jesting talking. wheat yields and bring forth good crop. Is not my word like as a fire and like a hammer that break the rock in pieces? Therefore I am against the prophets said the Lord, that steal my word every one his neighbor. they steal the truth from them and make them to believe a lie. behold I am against the prophet said the Lord that use their tongue and say he said, Jeremiah 23: 30. God said I sent them not nor commanded them. therefore they shall not profit this people at all.

So when these people or the prophets or the priest ask you, saying, what is the oracle of the Lord? You shall then say to them, What oracle? I will even forsake you, say the Lord. And as for the prophet and the priest and the people who say, the oracle of the Lord! I will even punish that man and his house. Thus every one of you shall say to his neighbor, and every one to his brother, What has the Lord answered? And, What has the Lord spoken?

And the oracle of the Lord you shall mention no more. forevery man's word will be his oracle, for you have perverted the word of the living God, the Lord of host, our God. But since you say, the oracle Lord! Therefore thus, said the Lord, because You say this word, the oracle of the Lord! I have sent you, saying, do not say, the oracle of the Lord!

Therefore behold, I even I, will utterly forget you and forsake you, and the city I gave you and your fathers, and will cast you out of my presence, and I will bring an everlasting reproach upon you, and a perpetual shame which shall not be forgotten.

Ezekiel 34:1-10 and the word of the lord came unto me saying, son of man prophesy against the shepherds of Israel, prophesy and say unto the shepherds of Israel that do feed themselves, should not they feed the flock? ye eat and fat and cloth you with wool, you kill them that are fed: but you feed not the flock. V-4, the diseased you have not strengthen, neither have you healed that which was sick, neither have you bounded up that which was broken, neither have you brought again that which was driven away, neither have you sort that which was lost.

Therefore you shepherds, hear the word of the Lord, as I live, said the Lord God, surely because my flock became a prey, and my flock became meat to every beast of the field, there were no shepherd neither did my shepherd search for the flock, but the shepherd fed themselves and feed not my flock.

The false prophets are used by the powers of darkness to lead the people of God back into bondage. This book enlighten you to know the difference between the true prophets of God and the counterfeit prophets. God said, I have not spoken to them yet they prophesy. but if they had stood in my counsel and caused my people to hear my words, then they would have turned from their wicked ways. Therefore O ye shepherds, hear the word of the Lord Thus said the Lord God, behold I am against the shepherd and I will require my flock at their hands and cause them to cease from feeding the flock neither shall the shepherd feed themselves any more, for I will deliver my flock from their mouth, that they may not be meat for them. my flock became meat to every beast of the field, because there was no shepherd. Ezekiel 34: 4-6

They were troubled because there were no shepherd, Zecharia10: 2. They build up Zion with blood and Jerusalem within equity, Micah 3:10. The head Judge for reward, and the priest teach for hire, and the prophets Divine for money: yet will they yet lean upon the Lord, and say are not the Lord among us? None evil shall come upon us. God will Judge among the people.

COUNTERFEIT PROPHET AND LEADERS FALL UNDER PRINCIPALITIES

Ephesians 6: 12

The counterfeit prophets are controlled by spiritual wickedness in high places. These counterfeits are responsible for the churches becoming weak and corrupted and brings false worship into the house of God. They bring in false teaching that causes err and misunderstanding among the believers. These spirits opens the door to occult powers and Soul prophesy and are used to gain one's own selfish purposes. I pray for God to enlighten your eyes of his people with understanding and wisdom. Titus 1:15-16 unto the all things are pure, in works they deny him.

Principalities are high racking demons who give orders to the lower rank demons, these demons are generals and give orders To destroy God Plans, they are controlling spirits and are assigned to the false prophets to bring the people of God under the influences of satanic powers.

* these spirits control the atmosphere.
* these spirits exalt themselves
* these spirits lie
* these spirits are selfish
* these spirits aggressive
* these spirits Influence mind of the people instead of God
* these spirits become Lord instead of God
* they bring pressure and oppression
* they bring carnality

* they bring insecurity
* they bring vain confidence
* they take away freedom replaces with control

These spirits causes the people to become dependent looking to them for deliverance, because of these spirits the church become weak and corrupt and are bought into false worship and false teaching which bring the people of God into err and confusion. these controlling spirits open the door to occult powers and self prophecy which are used to gain one's own selfish purpose, they are controlling spirits. when you discern these spirits you are commanded to cast them down.

Jezebel Spirit fall under the controlling spirits

This spirit hate the anointing. The Jezebel spirits are assigned to destroy those carry the anointing. they exalts position over the people of God. flesh against spirit. these Jezebel spirits desire their flesh to rule and dominate the spirit of God. they hate the prophets and all prophetic ministry. When Elijah killed the prophets of Baal, Jezebel sent word to him, she was going to take his life: 1king 19:1. These spirits use their power to intimidate the people, to gain power over them and bring them under a spirit of oppression. These spirits destroy the fruitfulness of others. They desire that the righteous people of God forsake their convictions. They are assigned to destroy the prophetic. The devil hate the prophetic flow of God, because the prophetic ministry demands repentance and cut away evil without compromise. The prophet always speak against Jezebel, the prophetic comes with creative power, which renders the enemy helpless. Jezebel threatened to take Elijah's life, fear arose and he fled, 1 King 19:1-6 The angel strengthen him, 19:7. Verse 15, God put him back into the race.

Jezebel spirits desires to paralyze the prophetic flow of God. When you recognize these spirits you are not to see yourself as a victim. Instead you are to stand up against them and cast them down and destroy their power. though prayer and commitment to truth and the willingness to confront lies. These spirits are determined and stubborn.

Elijah demands repentance, Jezebel hates repentance, Elijah demands righteousness Jezebel oppose righteousness, Elijah speak freedom, Jezebel desires control, Elijah demands humility, Jezebel appears to pride, Elijah speaks God's way, Jezebel uses deceit and system of witchcraft. Jezebel spirits usually work close to the Pastors, they work long and harder than anybody, they must always be the center attraction and in control, the chosen warriors are assigned to discern, defeat and confront the Jezebel These spirit cripples the church and operate with illegitimate authority. Jezebel spirits work in a person to manipulate, dominate and intimidate.

The church today is desperately in need of responsible leaders who are strong spiritual, and morally. We have many negative examples with powerful ministries. God does not want his people to faint in the heat of the battle, (Ephesians)3: 13, Paul said, I desire that ye faint not at my tribulation for you which is your glory. With out solid leaders, the people of God will spiritually faint and fall. When a Christian heart faints, he loses heart and stop fighting, they become weary and lose their strength. God leaders are the strength of the people.Standing is important to the weak, they depend on our spiritual walk with God.

Fainting bring weariness

Isaiah 40: 29-39, he give power to the faint and to them that have no might he increases strength, even the youth faint and be weary, and the young men utterly faint. But they that wait on the Lord he renews their strength, they shall mount up with wings of eagles they shall run and not be weary, they shall walk and not faint. God and his leaders are the ability, might, power, substance, force, security, stronghold and victory of the people. leaders must rely on God.

God Came To Deliver His People

God manifested in the flesh John Cha1, In the beginning was the word and the word was God and the word was with God. and the word John 1:14, the word was made flesh and dealt among us and we beheld the glory of the only begotten of the father full of grace and truth. For God so loved the world that he gave his only begotten son that whosoever believeth shall not perish but shall have ever lasting life.

Who are the believers? They are the chosen, John 15:16. The Lord know them that are his. John 10: I am the shepherd of the sheep, verse 9, I am the door, if any man enter in, he shall be saved. John10:3, Jesus called his sheep by name, the sheep heard the voice of Jesus and was led out of darkness into the marvelous light. John,10: 27, my sheep hear my voice I know them and they follow me.

God's Approval And Evidence To The Believer

Every believer must experience the water baptism of repentance John 3: 3-6, Jesus said to Nicodemus, verily, verily, I say unto you except a man be born again he cannot see the kingdom of God, verse 5, Except a man be born of the water and of the spirit he cannot enter into the kingdom of God. That which is born of the flesh is flesh and that which is born of the spirit is spirit.

Jesus was an example of the water baptism, he submitted to the holy spirit in obedience, Matt. 3:13. Jesus was baptized by John. Act1:5, until the day he was taken up, Jesus began to do and teach, after that the Holy Ghost had given commandments to the apostles whom he had chosen. he commanded them they should not depart from Jerusalem but wait for the promise of the father, for John truly baptized with water but ye shall be baptized with the Holy Ghost.

Act 2; 38, Peter said unto them repent, and be baptized every one of you in the name of Jesus for the remission of sins, and you shall receive the gift of the holy ghost. The day of Pentecost, God sent his holy spirit to his chosen people as the manifestation of his power and the assurance their identity Act 2:1-5 The Holy Ghost fell on each of them and they were all filled with the Holy Ghost and spoke with other tongue as the spirit of God gave them utterance. my sheep know my voice and I know them, and they follow me, John 10:27.

John 10: 28, Jesus said I give them eternal life and they shall never perish neither shall no man plunk them out of my hands, and the sheep follow me for they know my voice And a stranger will they not follow, but will flee from him for they know the voice of a stranger. concerning those who continue in fornication, God is your Judge, 1 Corinthian, 5: 1-5, he who has done this deed, even a son had his father's wife might be taken away from you to deliver such as one unto Satan for the destruction of the flesh that the spirit may be saved in the day of the Lord Jesus **Two thieves** were being hanged on the cross with Jesus, one of them mocked Jesus the other one said, doth not thy fear God, we receive due reward of our deeds but this man hath done nothing amiss, the thief said to Jesus, Lord, remember me when thy cometh into thy kingdom. And Jesus said unto him verily, I say unto thee today shall thy be with me in paradise. This man was a sinner but at the last hour he received Jesus as his Savior and was saved, what ever sin he has committed in his life time God forgave him on the cross, he was destined for eternal life.

My three brothers spent most of their lives on drugs and alcohol, Satan used them and destroyed their bodies but was not able to destroy their souls, God used me to lead them into the sinners prayers before their death at the last hour their souls were saved, they were destined for eternal life. Roman, 9: 18, Therefore he hath mercy on whom he will have mercy and whom he will he hardened.

Most of us are guilty of judging others, God said, judge nothing before the time. Judge not lest you be Judged Matt. 7:1. We all shall stand before the Judgment of God. God is the only one who has the power to Judge. Judge no one unless you be judged.

The Gift Of Tongue

Every one who receives the Holy Spirit must speak in tongues at lease once. The evidence is in Act Chapter 2, and when the day of Pentecost was fully come, They were all of one accord in one place. And suddenly there came a sound from heaven as of a mighty wind, and it filled all the house where they were sitting and there appeared unto them cloven tongues like as of fire and sat upon each of them and **they were all filled with the Holy Spirit and began to speak with other tongue as the spirit gave them utterance**. Some of you are given the gift of tongues and are able to speak often.

1 Corinthians, 12: 10, to another divers kind of tongues, to another interpretation of tongues: I Corinthians, 4:27, If any man speak in an unknown tongue, let it be by two, or three, and let one interpret. But if their be no interpreter, let him keep silent in the church, and let him

speak to himself and to God. 1 Corinthians 14:2, For he who speak in an unknown tongues speak not unto men, but unto God; for no man understand him.

1Corinthians 14:14, wherefore let him that speak in an unknown tongue pray that he may interpret. 1 Corinthians 14:14, for if I pray in an unknown tongue my spirit pray, but my understanding is unfruitful. Verse 15, what is it then? I will pray with the Spirit, and I will pray with the understanding also. Or when thy bless with the spirit, how shall he who occupy the room of the unlearn say amen, seeing he understand not what you say or what you pray.

1 Corinthians 13 1-13, Paul said, Thou I speak with the tongues of men and of angels having not charity, [love] I am becoming as a sounding brass, or a tinkling cymbal and thou I have gifts of prophecy and all knowledge and though I have faith so that I can move mountains and have not charity, I am nothing. I Corinthians 14:4-6, I would that ye all speak with tongue but rather that ye prophesied for greater is he that prophesied than he that speak with tongues, except he interpret, that the church may receive edifying.

Verse 4, he that speak in an unknown tongue edify himself, but he that prophesy edify the church. Verse 6, Paul said, Now brethren, If I come unto you speaking with tongues, what shall I profit you, except I shall speak to you either by revelation, or by knowledge, or by prophesying, or by doctrine, Verse 18, I thank my God, I speak with tongue more than you all, I had rather speak five words with understanding than ten thousand words in an unknown tongue that I might teach others. 1 Corinthians 14:4-6, V-18. Satan also has a tongue, his tongue is counterfeit. Alter workers you must be able to discern Satan tongue from the Holy Spirit, The alter is a Holy place, those of you working the alter should be full of the Holy Ghost: many people come to the alter for delivered from demons. You must be prepared for this Job which calls for a consecrated life.

COMMUNION

God principles in taking communion

Communion has been provided by God, only for the born again believers, communion is not for your unsaved children, only if they have been born again. before the children are twelve years of age their sins are upon the parent; God holds you responsible for their sins, after the age of twelve they are responsible for their own sins. Communion is not for sinners, but has been prepared for believers. We must understand every body does not have the same privilege as born again believers.

1Corinthians 11:28-30 but let a man examine himself and so let him eat bread and drink of the cup, For he who eats and drinks of an unworthy manner eats and drinks judgment to himself, not discerning the Lord's body. For this reason many are weak and sick among you, and many sleep, {dead }This indicates that some are sick and some are dead; because they did not examine themselves and they judged the body in a wrong manner. When we do not discern the body of Christ with his compassion and unconditional love and mercy, we are out of order with his word. 1 Corinthians 11:24 and when he had given thank, he brake it and said, take, eat, this is my body which is broken for you this do in remembers of me.

Communion is pure and sacred, those who abuse it will pay the consequences. The price paid for the abuse is sickness or death. Communion is to be taken in a serious manner without hypocrisy; repentance is important beforehand.

JESUS THE GOOD SHEPHERD

John, 10: 11, I am the good shepherd, the good shepherd give his life for his sheep. He expect us to give up our fleshly desires to serve him.

Jesus of compassion

Matthew 15: 32, The compassion of Jesus for the multitude. I have compassion on them because they continued with me now three days, and have nothing to eat, I will not send them away Fasting, Lest they faint on the way. He loved his people and did great things for them yet they were ungrateful, they flattered him with their mouth and lied to him with their tongue, their heart was far from him Verse 8, but he being full of compassion forgave them their iniquity and destroyed them not.

Ps. 86:15, but thy, o Lord, art a God full of compassion, and gracious, longsuffering and plenteous mercy and truth. Isaiah 49:15, Can a woman forget her sucking child, that she should not have compassion on the son of her womb? Yea, they may forget, yet will I not forget thee. Matthew 9:36, but when he saw the multitude, he was moved with compassion on them, because they fainted, and were scattered abroad, as sheep having no shepherd. Matthew 20: 34, Jesus had compassion on them and touched their eyes and immediately their eyes received sight, and they followed him. Luke 7: 17, and when the Lord saw her, he had compassion on her, and said weep not, he touched her dead son and he sat up and began to speak and he delivered him to his mother.

1 Peter 3:8, finally, be ye all one mind, having compassion one of another, and love as brethren.1 John 3:17, but whosoever hath this world goods, and see his brother and shut his bowel of compassion from him how dwell the love in him. Compassion is to have pity and mercy and sympathy on another. Whenever we see an individual in need, if we are able to do so, we are to have compassion.

Jesus And Meekness

Jesus was meek and humble, he humbled himself under the hand of the all mighty God. Moses was a meek above all the men who were on the face of the earth. Blessed are the meek for they shall inherit the earth. the meek shall eat and be satisfied. The meek will he guide in judgment and the meek will he teach his way. Numbers Cha. 12. Matt. 5:5. Ps. 22:26. Ps.25:9.

The Meek Shall Inherit The Earth

The Lord lift up the meek. The Lord will beautify the meek with salvation. for I am meek and lowly in heart. But let the hidden man of the heart in which is not corruptible, even the ornament of a quiet meek and quiet spirit, which is in the sight of God of great price, meekness is one of the fruit given to us from the Holy Spirit, Meekness does not represent weakness but is a form of humility unto God, Therefore humble your self under the almighty hands of God and he will exalt you in due time. Ps. 37:11. Ps147:4. Ps. 149:4. 1 Peter 3:4. Galatians 5: 22.

Wisdom

To know wisdom and instruction. To perceive the words of understanding, a wise man will hear and increase learning and a wise man will hear and will increase learning. a man of understanding shall attain unto wise counsels. The fear of the Lord is the beginning of wisdom but fools despise wisdom and instruction. My son, forget not my law. but let thy heart keep commandments. For length of days and long life, and peace, they shall add to thee, so shall thy fine favor and good understanding in the sight of God and man. Proverb,1:2-7. Proverb Cha.3.

Verse 5, Trust in the Lord with all thy heart and lean not unto thy own understanding. In all thy ways acknowledge him and he shall direct thy path. Be not wise in thy own eyes. fear the Lord, and depart from evil. My son despise not the chastening of the Lord neither be weary of his correction, Verse 13. Happy is the man that fine wisdom, and the man that get understanding. Wisdom is more precious than rubies. Verse 18, wisdom is a tree of life to them that lay hold upon her. And happy is every one that retain her. Proverb Verse 20. My son attend to my words incline thy ear unto my word, keep them in your heart. Don't ever let any one remove God's word from your heart, guard it.

Trust is earned though love. It's impossible to trust some one, who does not love you. Jesus love speak to us from the cross. Every one of us should be convinced of his love, we can trust him with all of our heart, knowing our trust is safe. The wisdom of God Is to obey without human understanding and with out sight.

ACTION OF THE GREAT SHEPHERD

To all spiritual shepherds though out all ages, the proper attitudes and Actions

* Searched out the lost sheep
* Deliver the captive sheep
* Gather the dispersed sheep
* Comfort the weary sheep
* Bounded up the hurt sheep
* Strengthened the weak sheep
* Guided the direction of the sheep
* Carry the broken sheep
* restored the soul of the tired sheep
* comforted the agitated sheep
* prepared the table for the frightened sheep.

The Shepherd is the Watchman

Ezekiel 3: 17, Ezekiel 33: 3-7, Isaiah 62: 6: Jeremiah 6: 17

Isaiah 21: 5-8, natural shepherd watches over their flock, God expect his leaders to watch over his flock and to warn them of danger, such as lions, bears, lamb or a wounded sheep, vultures are eagles they will swoop down to wound the young of the flock and return later for the kill. The shepherd must be a far seeing watchman and must be alert to danger around the flock, he or she dare not be lazy or an unseen watchman. The leader must be a watchman. the church has many enemies that will attack the house of God in the last days. lazy shepherds leave the church open to attacks counterfeit shepherds who has inflicted some of the worst wounds on the people of God. The church is the hope of protection. The sheep look to the shepherd as a guide, to guide them into a new life of truth.

The Shepherd Is The Protector

The shepherd is a guard, a protector and a defender of the flock without a shepherd the sheep would wander aimlessly until they died of starvation or thirst. the lives of the sheep depends on his guidance. sheep are sensitive and cannot endure hard driving. some weak, sickly or injured sheep would die if the shepherd drove them too far or too fast they are meant to be led gently. A shepherd should guide his flock with tender, sensitivity, gentleness, observation and patience, the church of the Lord Jesus has many young and tender sheep, these cannot be driven hard by forceful men, They must be gently guided by true shepherds.

The shepherd Is a Physician

The shepherd is a physician who heal relieve and comfort his sheep repairing broken hearts and wounded spirits, this is the work of the true shepherds who has a shepherds heart. The spiritual shepherd must have spiritual discernment regarding problems that overtake the flock. Jesus concerned about hurting sheep:

Matthew 9:12, they that be whole need not a physician but they who are sick. Multitudes of sick people are in the church today who need a physician, only a true shepherd can to heal the flock, though the word of God, Jesus is the physician: God and only he is qualified to give the increase, all that we do come from the power of God, working in us and though us.

The Concept Of A Hireling Shepherd

Labors only for money Matthew20: 17
Has no heart for the people
Leaves when trouble come Jeremiah 46: 22
Is unfaithful to his master
Feeds himself and not the sheep Ezekiel 34: 3

Neglect the sheep
Lack of mercy Ezekiel 34:4
Is harsh, cruel, and forceful
Drives the sheep too hard
Is not willing to make personal sacrifices Ezekiel: 34:2
Is ambitious for position, but avoids responsibility
Does not take the time to bind up the sheep's wounds
Domineers the sheep
Does not care about the sheep needs
Produce unfaithfulness in the sheep
Is anxious at the close of the day
Makes no personal investment in the sheep
Has no balance in discipline, to harsh or not at all
Limit his work to a given time period (Isaiah)16: 14, 21: 16
Forget the lost of them driven away
Is a work of men's hands PS,135: 15-18, 115: 4-
Has a mouth that speak not
Has eyes that see not
Has ears that hear not
Has hands that do not touch or feel.

Apostle Paul said in Act Cha 20, I know that after my departure savage wolves will come in among you not sparing the flock. Some of you will distort the truth in order to draw disciples unto yourselves. This is the time. Jesus said in the book of revelation, he who has an let him ear hear what the spiritual of the lord is saying to the churches.

The True Shepherd's Heart male and female

Labor of love
Has the heart of God
Gives his life for the sheep, John 10:11 (giving up their own desires)
Faithfully serves his master
Feeds the sheep
Tenderly cares for the sheep
gentle kind and loving
Leads the people wisely
Unites the sheep
Is always willing to make personal sacrifices.

Is not oriented to position, but has a servants heart
Binds the brokenhearted
Leads the sheep lovely
Discern the needs of the sheep
Causes the sheep to be fruitful
Is peaceful and watchful (especially at night)
Receiving the flock of God as his inheritance
Invest their life in the sheep at the highest price he can pay
Disciplines with the rod and the staff of God in love
Gives himself to his work full time, it is his calling and his life style
Seek out the lost and those driven away
Is a work of Gods hands
Has a mouth that has speak spiritual things
Has eye to discern spiritual things
Has ears to hear spiritual things
Produces his same feelings, discerning and spiritual nature in the people

May every spiritual shepherd forsake the way of the hireling and truly shepherd the flock of God.

God speaks to his prophets concerning his people

for thus said the Lord God, behold I, even I will both search my sheep and seek them out, Ezekiel 34:11-4. I will feed them in green pastors and upon the high mountains of Israel shall their fold be they shall lie down in green pasture, Ps. 23 and I will give you Pastors according to my heart which shall feed you with knowledge and understanding, Jeremiah 3:15.

And I will make them a place round about my hill a blessing, and I will cause the shower to come down in his season there shall be showers of blessings. and the trees of the field shall yield her fruit, and the earth shall yield her increase and they shall be safe in the land and shall know that I am the Lord,

Ezekiel 34: 6+ V-27.

I will break the bands of their yoke and delivered them out of the hands of those who serve themselves of them, and they shall no more be a prey to the heathen, neither shall the beast of the land devour them, they shall dwell safely and none shall make them afraid, and ye my flock, God has commanded us from his word, Isaiah to open the blinded eyes, to bring out the prisoners and those who sit in darkness out of the prison house, Isaiah 42: 7.

We have not received the spirit of the world, but the spirit of God that we might know the things that are free given to us of God, the holy ghost teaches, comparing spiritual things with spiritual. The natural man cannot receive the spiritual things of God, he cannot know them because they are spiritually discerned. God said, I show my secrets unto my prophets. he reveals to us the secret of his treasury. he promised if we seek him we shall find him, to find something you must search for it: Gods word is a treasure it is more valuable than silver and gold It gives life, health and prosperity, 1 Corinthians 2:12-1.

Seed On the Good Ground

God created Adam and Eve from the earth; all life must come forth from a seed: a seed must be planted. Before any human life is formed, it has to start from a seed. After the seed has been planted, it must to be nourished whether it's human life, fruit and vegetable life, animal life or insect life, all life began with a seed planted. From each of these life forms, some of these will come forth good and some corrupted.

But he who receive seed on good ground, is he that hear the word and understand it, which also bear fruit and bring forth a hundred, some sixty, some thirty, this group hear the word and receive it. Jesus is the true vine, we are the branches. Every branch that bear fruit, (you) he purged it that it may bring forth more fruit, he that abide in me and I in him, the same bright forth fruit, for without me you can do nothing. herein is my father glorified that you bear much fruit. these things have I spoken unto you, that my joy remain in you and that your joy be full. Matt, 13:23. John cha,15:2-11.

Now you are clean though the word which I have spoken to you. verse, you are my friends, if you do whatsoever I command you. Henceforth, from this point on I call you not servants, for the servant do not know what his Lord doeth. but I have called you friends. Jesus said, all things that I have heard of my father I have made it known unto you. But I have chosen you and ordained you to go forth and bring forth fruit and your fruit shall remain: if any man come after me he must first deny himself: except a corn of wheat fall into the ground and die, it abide alone. But if it die, it bring forth much fruit, John 15: 3. John 13:16.

John 12:24. John 14:16. Before bringing forth fruit your flesh has to die.

If any man serve me, let him follow me, where I am there shall also my servant be; {be where?} **in the spirit;** and if any man serve me, him will my father honor. for the time cometh, and now is, when the true worshipers shall worship the father in spirit and in truth, for the father seek such to worship him. **For God is a spirit and they that worship (must)worship him in spirit and in truth.** God has commanded our lives to become a worship of holiness: children of God we must bring forth the fruit of holiness, John4:23+24.

John: Cha. 15: 18 + 19, if the world hate you it hated me before it hated you, if you were of the world the world would love you, but because you are not of the world, the world hate you, because God has chosen us out of the world. The good seed will constantly have warfare with the bad seed, the bad seed are the tares, the children of the devil, they hate you because you are the good Seed and are chosen by God, Satan and his demons hate the fact of losing their place in heaven, we have taken their place, their wrath is warfare.

The word of God said when the good seed came up, the bad seed, which are the tares came up together with the good seed, Satan is a counterfeit, he counterfeit the bad seed to look identically to the good seed. Many times the sheep are attacked because they are unable to discern the bad seed from the good seed, God has chosen watchman on the wall to protect the sheep. God has also given you in his word to know to know the difference between the good and bad seed, you shall know them by their fruit, a good tree does not bear bad fruit but bear good fruit. It is impossible for the bad seed to bear good fruit: demons are bad fruit.

SPIRITUAL WICKEDNESS
IN HIGH PLACES EXPOSED

Satan kingdom is a well organized kingdom with millions of demons they are waiting to take orders to do battle against the people of God, against ministries against families against marriages against cities against states and against nations. Satan was not in control of Jesus death; God was completely in charge of the death of Jesus; it was the will of God. Pilate said, to the leaders, you have a custom that I should release unto you one at the Passover, the king of the Jews or Barabbas. Demons cried out of the people, release to us Barabbas. Satan influenced the people to chose Barabbas who was a robber, John Cha.18.

Even though the voices of the people were heard, the vicious cries came forth from demons. Pilate said behold your king, the demons cried out and said, away with him, away with him, crucify him. Demons spoke out of Pilate again and said, I have the power to crucify you and the power to release you. John 14+15, Jesus said, you have no power at all against me except it were given you from my father. God used Satan to bring Jesus into his destiny. God declare all thing are working together to accomplish his will. God is using Satan to bring you into your destiny. God has given us to triumph over our enemy into victory. God is exalted Satan is defeated.

Spiritual Wickedness In High Places Are Responsible

Malice the deliberate intention of doing unjustified harm for the satisfaction of doing it.

Jealousy felling a spiteful envy toward someone more successful than oneself.

Illness an unhealthy condition of body or mind

Murder to kill a person physically or character

Suicide the act of taking one's own life

Drugs Substance abuse

Outburst Eruption, violent expression of feeling

Dissensions disagreement in opinion, discord, Quarreling

Contentions incline to find reasons for contention over unimportant matters.

Principalities Are Assigned To All Abuses

Wife abuse, child abuse, animal abuse

These spirits are order by the high ranking spirits, Principalities:

If any of these abuse demon are assigned to any member of your family

Fast and pray and cast them down. the anointing destroys the yoke:

We are commanded to pray for sinners, backsliders, youth, children and all saints bind the abuse demons in the name of Jesus and cast them out and loose those who are bounded. God is calling for the intersession prayer warriors, pray and brings deliverance to the people. You may not see result right away, God will answer, thou the vision tarry wait for It, it shall speak. You faith is planting a seed for someone's deliverance.

Uncompromising word of God.

The word of God is powerful as any two edge sword, God word is alive it should not be compromised, it is the power of God unto salvation, when it is preached it either draw or drive, the word of God will deliver those who receive it.

Satan know the word, but it is the power in the word he fears, It is written, the letter kill but the spirit bring life. Paul said, I do not seek to please men but God. if I please men I cannot please God. all saints must have the same attitude, either you will be a man pleaser or a God pleaser.

Corinthians 3:10-15, God has given to us his grace as a wise master builder, Paul said, I have laid the foundation and another build thereon, but let every him take heed how he build thereupon. No other foundation can be laid only the foundation which Jesus Christ has laid. if any man build upon silver, gold, precious stones, wood, hay stubble, every man's work shall be manifest, for the day shall declare it, because it shall be revealed by fire and the fire shall try every man's work of what sort it is, the fire will test and critically appraise the character and worth of the work each person has done.

If any man's work abide he has built on this foundation, he shall receive a reward, but if any man's work is burned up under the test, he will suffer the lost, losing his reward though he himself shall be saved, but only as one who passed through the fire, for he know the way that I take when I am tried I shall come forth as pure gold. My foot hath held my steps, his way have I kelp, and not declined, neither have I gone back from the commandment of his lips. I have esteemed the words of his mouth more than my necessary food. Verse 8, every man shall receive his own reward. all the building fitly framed together grow unto an holy temple in the Lord in whom ye are build together for an habitation of God though the Spirit, Job 23:10-12.

Who shall separate us from the love of God? Shall tribulation, (no), distress (no), persecution (no), famine (no) shall if God be for us who can be against us? Who shall separate us from the love of God, nakedness (no), peril (no), or sword (no). nay in all things we are more than conquerors though him that loved us, for I am persuaded that neither death nor life nor angels nor principalities nor powers nor things present, nor things to come nor height, nor depth, nor any other creature, shall be able to separate us from the love of God, which is in Christ Jesus Our Lord.

Demons in the work place
The power of fasting

Fasting destroys the yokes of the enemy, and is a weapon against him. Jesus fasted 40 days for preparation against temptation in the wilderness.

in that day the burden shall be taken away from off thy neck and the yoke shall be destroyed because of the anointing. the anointing destroy the yoke in the work place. Isaiah 43. Isaiah 58:6. If you are a beginner in fasting, you can start fasting two or three hour a day and add more hour as you progress. Even thou you are fasting, watch for Satan he will show up, the word on him, 2 Corinthians 10: 4 he will flee. The word of God is like fire to Satan, it burns up his plans.

The price for the anointing is sacrifice. Know ye not that your body is the temper of the Holy Ghost: If any man come after me he must first deny him self pick up his cross and follow me. Matthew 10:37, he that love father, mother, son or daughter more than me is not worthy of me. John 14:21, he that keep my commandments he it is who love me and he shall be love of my father, I will love him and will manifest my self to him.

Phil 3:10, that I might know him in the power of his resurrection, and the fellowship of his suffering, being conformable unto his death. For whosoever shall lose his life for my sake shall find it. John 14: 22-23: being tested in the fire, giving up your will to please God. The disciples asked Jesus a question, how is it that thou will manifest thyself unto us and not the world? Jesus said if a man love me he will keep my words and my father will love him and we will come unto him and make our abode with him.

Some of the Ways of God manifesting himself to us:

working his power though us

* casting out demons
* healing the sick
* answers to prayers
* healing our bodies
* delivering our children
* working miracles
* opening blinded eyes
* the lame to walk, dumb to talk

God declare in his word, his hears are open to the righteous and he answers our Prayers. God manifested his miracle power to me as I was in spiritual warfare for a young man. Satan attack this young man and tried to set him up. He was locked up in jail, they were trying to give him 25 to life, my staff and I went before the Lord in fasting and praying, we laid before God in fasting faith and praying for months, God worked a supernatural miracle, the case were closed God delivered him and set him free. It was a miracle. Though this miracle, God Drew this young Man in and turned his life around and is blessing him exceeding and Abundantly and above all he would think or ask, the glory go to God.

God work miracles

Exodus Cha.4, God's miracle: Moses rod became a serpent
Verse 6, God turned Moses hand leprous as snow and turned it back to flesh.

Satan work miracles

Pharaoh rods became serpents, Pharaoh miracles was operated by Satan. Satan can work miracles: he will work miracles during the tribulation: God warns you in his word, believe not every but try the spirit and see whether it be of God. Many false Christ has gone into the world. Revelation Cha.13, John saw a beast was wounded and died Satan worked a miracle and brought the beast back to life, because of Satan's deception, all the world worshiped the beast and said who is like unto the beast.

People of God night is far spent, the time of the Lord is at hand. God is saying to you gird up the lions of your mind stop running after Idol god they cannot save you from the wrath of God.

Stop running after miracle, run after God. every miracle is not from God. God has warned you, do not to walk by sight but walk by faith. Timothy Cha 1, hold fast the form of sound words, which thy has heard of me, in faith and love which is in Christ Jesus. John 12: 35, Jesus is saying to you, yet a little while is the light with you, walk in the light lest darkness come upon you: for he who walk in the darkness know not where he goes. Believe in the light that you may be children of the light. Why should you believe a lie rather than the truth. God's word is true those who do not believe the truth, God said, he sent them a strong delusion to believe a lie other then the truth.

<Four things Satan uses to enslave you>

* The pride of life—putting material things before God
* The lust of the flesh
* The lust of the eye
* The cares of this world

Flee these things, recognize them, resist them, run from them, do not be persuaded, say no to them, do not entertain them.

Matt.19: 22, those who received seed by the way side and those who receive seed in stony places, are deceived by the enemy.

Weapons To Use In Warfare

having on the breast plate of righteous doing that which is right

Fear is the opposite of faith

Fear is strong emotion caused by expectation, anxious concern.

Isaiah 41:10-14 fear thou not; for I am with you: be not dismayed for I am thy God: I will strengthen you and help you. I the Lord your God will hold your right hand fear not I will help you.

Above all taking the shield of faith

You shall be able to quench all the fiery dart of the wicked when Satan attack you with doubt and fear, attack him with the sword of the spirit and the weapon of faith without faith it is impossible to please God, the entire bible is based on faith. faith is the key word in winning the battle. Hebrew11:1, from the amplified bible, faith is the assurance, the confirmation, the title deed of the things we hope for, being the proof of things we do not see and the conviction of the reality. Faith perceiving as real fact what is not revealed to our senses, not seeing but believe.

The Helmet Of Salvation

is the assurance of your faith, 1John, 5:11, this is the record that God has given us eternal life in his son, the helmet protects your head, mind and your thoughts from false teachings and gives confidence and boldness in conflict to go forward into battle.

Sword of the spirit

the word of God is sword sharper than any two edge sword.

Powers Of Prayer

A very important weapons in spiritual warfare is prayer, God said pray always with out ceasing.

Your mind Is The Battle Field

2 Corinthians10:4,The weapon of your warfare is not carnal but mighty through God to the pulling down of strong hold and casting down every imagination and every high thing that will exalt itself against the knowledge of God and bringing every thought unto the obedience of Christ. A strong hold Is a place having a strong defense, the strong place Satan has build in your mind: We are to pull down every strong hold from our minds and build our strong defense against the enemy.

when Satan attack your body with sickness, your defense is the word of God. I am healed by Jesus stripes. When he attack your mind with confusion, your defense is, God has not given me the spirit of fear but love power and a sound mind. as you resist Satan he will flee.

Your Flesh Is An Enemy

Paul Said I want to do good but to perform that which is good I find not. If I do that, it is not I but the sin in me, Paul said, I want to do right, but there is another law in my members, warring against the law of my mind and bringing me into captivity to the law of sin, o wretched man that I am, who shall deliver me from the body of death? I thank God though Jesus Christ our Lord, with my mind I serve the law of God, but with the flesh the law of sin. Though the blood of Jesus we are free from the law, no longer are we bounded by the flesh. For they that are after the flesh do mind the things of the flesh, but they that are after the spirit the things of the spirit, Roman Cha 7. Roman Cha, 8.

To be carnal minded is death. book of Roman, but to be spiritual minded is life and peace, so then they that are after the flesh cannot please God. Do not feed your flesh: starve the flesh and feed your spirit. Train your mind in the word Speak the word, believe the word, walk in the word, decree the word declare the word, sleep on the word, remain spiritual aware in the word, until Satan understand that is the mind of Christ, and they are forbidden from your mind, even though Satan has access into your mind, he cannot control it unless you allow it, greater is he in you than he in the world, his name is Jesus.

Work of the flesh

The works of the flesh are these: Adultery, fornication uncleanness, lasciviousness, idolatry, witchcraft, hatred, variance, emulation, wrath, strife, sedition, heresies, envying, murders, rebellion drunkenness, those who do shall not enter in the kingdom of God, Your spirit is saved but not your flesh, you are a sinner saved by grace but you have the power over your flesh though the blood of Jesus. You must constantly fast bringing your flesh under subjection to the Holy Spirit: Paul understood the important of fasting, he said after I have preached to others I must bring my flesh under subjection otherwise I myself will become a castaway.

Two Powerful Spiritual weapons

The weapon of holiness and righteousness carry strength and light and are given to you by the Holy Spirit. Satan recognizes the light, it reminds him of his office in heaven as a light bearer but now he walks in darkness he and his demons scream at the sight of light, light destroys all darkness Matt 5:14, you are the light of the world a city that is set on a hill cannot be hid neither do men light a candle and put it under a bushel but on a candle stick and it give light to all in the house. Let your light so shine before men, that they may see your good works and glorify your father which is in heaven. The people who sat in darkness saw a great light and to them who sat in the region and shadow of death. You become a threat to Satan because of the light you carry, Matt 4:14.

Arise And Shine

Isaiah 60:1, arise and shine for the light has come and the glory of the Lord is risen upon thee. For behold, the darkness shall cover the earth and gross darkness the people, but the Lord shall arise upon thee, and his glory shall be seen upon thee. Your heart shall swell with joy, the abundant of the sea shall turn to you and the wealth of the gentiles shall come to you. The anointing shall be seen on you, the glory of God is the anointing. Our God shall shine forth in those who keep his covenant.

Principalities:

Chief magistrates over cities, states, nations. They are top general who give orders, the most important assignment orders is to destroy the church, the people of God, the body of Christ.

Powers

controlling spirits who bring a person satanic influences. These demons bring in vain imagination and seducing spirits, They exalt themselves and influences the though life.

Rulers Of The Darkness Of This World:

these demons are master world rulers who govern countries, states and cities, They are antichrist spirits that draw people away from Christ.

Spiritual Wickedness In High Place

These spirits causes malice, pain, hurt, illness, disease, depression, fear, poverty, and all oppression among the people, the angles of light, the tares, Satan's ministers and the false prophets are controlled by spiritual wickedness in high places. The false prophets, the false prophets are controlled by these spirits and causes the church to become weak and corrupt, and brings false worship into the house of God and false teaching that brings in err and misunderstanding among the believers.

These spirits also open the door to occult power and hold the people of God in a yoke of bondage, these spirits are also Jezebel spirits, Jezebel spirits must be the center attention. When the people are held in bondage it gives them a carnal security and vain confidence. These spirits controls their minds and emotions causing them to serve the flesh, bringing them into false worship. They are hindering spirits, they are designed to hinder the progress of God. these demons work from the heavens and are given orders from principalities. These mind demons are strong affective. Determent and violent. They have defiled the dwelling place of God's name to the ground. They despise the spirit of God and those determined to stand firm in the anointing. Their fight is over power, they will do any thing necessary achieve their goals.

Wrestle

to throw or swing, is a contest between two opponents that continues until one hurls the other one down and holds him down, only one will win, ether you or Satan, you are wrestling with a personal foe, face to face, hand to hand, conflict to the finish, the warfare will not end until you have won the victory over every area of your life, your mind, emotion, flesh, and your body. these are the areas Satan is fighting to control. You must use your weapons to protect your territory and control the atmosphere of your surroundings, you are never to retreat in the time of battle.

Operation of Demons

One third of the angles were cast out of heaven with Lucifer. There names are now demons, they are evil spirits who inhabit the bodies of human being, they use those who are disobedient and reject God. they influence baby saints for a season during their testing, once the baby saint is mature Satan has to flee.

Satan can use these against you

* employees on your job
* family
* church members
* individuals in your neioborhood
* next door neioborhood
* husband
* wife
* children
* friends
* boss on your job

Demons are at work. but can only survive in a human body. They use a vessels who are open to their wickedness. These demons operates in the house of God. God commands his people to watch fast and pray and cast them out of individuals whom they possess in the house of God. Peter 5:8, be sober and vigilant because your adversary the devil is roaring like a lion walking about seeking to whom he may devoir. God has commanded the body of Christ to know the difference Gal 5:22+ 23,we shall know them by their fruit, they will either produce the works of the flesh or the fruit of the spirit: Ephesians 6: 12 as you read this book you will learn the important of following the instructions of the holy spirit.

Beware of transferring of spirits

Take heed to the word of God, transference of spirits can come though laying on of hands. before laying on hands or casting out demons be sure you are chosen and anointed by the Holy Spirit to work in these areas. Prayer and fasting is very important. Matt 17:19, the disciples asked Jesus why could we not cast out the demons? Jesus said because of your unbelief. verse 21, this kind goes out only by prayer and fasting.

Transferring of spirits can be transferred to others in the misted of a deliverance service as demons are being cast out. Before a deliverance service of casting out demons, the audience should be prayed over and covered in the blood of Jesus. The person who are in charge of the service must have the anointing of God on their life and those working with him. These spirits can come though a lust spirit or any unclean spirit, they can transform onto a weak saint or children. If an unauthorized person {such as a counterfeit Christian} lay hands on some one who need deliverance, he will transfer spirits on to that person.

These spirits will transfer on to them or in them: before getting hands laid on you, be sure to chose a true anointed woman or man of God for your deliverance. A counterfeit Christian is one who rejects Christ. Usually they are adulterers, committing fornication or doing some kind of sin without repentance or they are touching some unclean thing. The word of God said touch not the unclean thing and I will receive you. The unclean person is not receive by God, they themselves are possessed with demon spirits. Saint of God you must be alert.

Imagination

Roman 1.21

Because when they knew God they glorified him not as God neither were thankful but became vain in their imagination and their foolish hearts were darkened. professing themselves to be wise they became fools and changed the glory of God uncorrupt into an image made like to corruptible man where God gave them up to uncleanness through the lust of their own heart to dishonor their own bodies between themselves, sexual act between two men or two woman.

Close the door to evil spirits

We close the door to evil when we obey God, we open the door to evil when we reject God.

Roots:

A root is something that become fixed, take root, a weak area that identifies the beginning of a hurt or wound in our life. Stop the cycle and admit your hurt and shameful feelings, forgive and repent of your wrong fillings, recognize your fear of authority figure and fear of being embarrassed publicly. The thing we fear some times draws that very thing to us.

Ask God to heal your self-image and worth and also heal the self hate toward your self, the spirit of intimidation which is tormenting you, command it to leave in the name of Jesus. Fear is a major root problem that works with the devils strategies, because fear is the opposite of faith, the enemy uses fear as a tactic to open areas of weakness in us. the spirit of fear is one of Satan major strong holds. Unless this strong hold is pulled down it will take root. Fear falls under spiritual wickedness Ephesians cha.6, 11 Tim. 1:7, For God has not given us the spirit of fear but love power and a sound mind, ask your self a question, who sent the spirit of fear? Satan in responsible, this is one of Satan's most powerful weapons, he controls using fear as his weapon: God's word to you, do not fear. You have the power to all demonic spirits and cast them all out, do not allow them to take root.

Spirit of haughtiness

Proverb 6:18, pride goes before a fall and destruction and a haughty spirit before a fall, manifestations of this spirit is pride self exaltation, domineering, gossip, lofty, stubbornness, arrogance, boastful, bragging, self righteousness, failure to examine oneself, religiousness, man's tradition, scornful, being critical others, haughtiness perverted pride thinking too low of ones self, false humility conceited pride and thinking too highly of oneself.

Spirit of mammon

Luke 12: 14, 1 Thessalonians 2:5, 6, Hebrew 13: 5. let your character be free from the love of money, being content with what you have. what limit will you go to obtain money and wealth, will you disobey God's principles to get it? Do you love money more than you love God? Matthew. 6: 24 says no man can serve two masters, for he will hate the one and love the other or he will hold to the one and despise the other. You can not serve God and mammon.

Webster's dictionary defines mammon as riches regarded as a object of worship and greedy pursuit wealth or material gain as an evil. manifestation are. Greed, pride, selfishness, lust, lying, deceptions, dishonesty. The word of God says the love of money is the root of all evil, Wealth and having money is not evil, the evil is loving money more than God is the evil, it becomes an idol and becomes evil mammon falls under the rulers of darkness in Ephesians Cha 6 if you love money more than God you are an enemy to God. Either you are an enemy of God or a friend of God.

Spirit of error +religion

1 John 4:6, says, we are from God, he who know God listen to us, he who is not from God does not listen to us, we are the children of God only those who have walked and talked with God will listen to us. by this we know the spirit of truth and the spirit of err. 1 Tim. 6:3-10, James 5:19-20, Rom. 13:7-9, 1 Tim. 1:13-11, James 1: 26-27, Act 13: 35-50. Luke 6: 2,7. Luke 12: 56, 20:1-2. John 2: 14-16.

The Pharisees were religious, they taught the law but disobeyed them constantly. They were always accusing Jesus, and hated his disciples. They were hypocrites and had no desire to change. Matt. Cha. 12, the Pharisees accursed the disciples. Religious causes strife, jealousy, contradictions, arguing, love of money, selfish gain, abuse of God's people, after their own financial gain, control of the people of God and the stifling of the gifts of the Holy spirit.

Though out the old testament we see, the Scribes and Pharisees wanted to put Jesus to death because of their religious belief and the spirit of err. The spirit of religion works with lying spirits and cause one not to hear or speak the correct information or to see the word of God correctly, when we come against religion and the spirit of err we are to command the spirit of err to be broken in Jesus name and cast it down.

Manipulation

This spirit brings selfish motion. People who manipulate get others to do things for benefiting themselves rather than the one who is being manipulated, it is pressure to take away some one's choice. Manipulation does not benefit both parties, only the one who is doing the manipulating. Manipulation is control. manipulation and control causes Churches to be weak, divided, discord, slander, causing the people of God to lose sight on God and began to idolize people instead of God. They become more committed to the person than to God Some times fear and jealous work together with this spirit. This spirit lies, cheat and misuse others.

The people of the world and some church people use this spirit to manipulate. Those who use this spirit are prospering in material things, but their souls are not prospering, they have gain riches and wealth but have rejected the Son of God; they are miserable and without peace.

Many have left God because of the love of money, their money has become their god: the bible said it is appointed for man to die and then the judgment, when a person die he will not be able to take things with him, such as drivers license, credit cards nor riches or wealth. the last thing seen on the dead body is the clothes and the casket they are laying in, those things will turn to dust with the body.

The clothes, caskets and your body will return back to the earth. the soul will either rest with God or be tormented in hell until the judgment. Those who rejects Christ will end up in the lake of fire. Revelation 20: 15, and Whoever was not found written in the book of life was cast into the lake of fire.

This spirit of manipulation is used to gain one's own selfish gain. This spirit works together with the mind control spirit and the Jezebel spirit. Its subject is the mind, the emotions, and the will to serve flesh and brings worship to a person and not to God, this spirit demands its own way, it is harsh, bossy and aggressive, it gives soul Prophecy and causes the people to be drawn to them instead of drawing to God, This spirit cause the people to fill inadequate, it hinders some from succeeding and cripples others, people under these spirits are confused, frustrated, fearful, immature, weak, not motivated and lose their dream, the people has been drawn into the spirit of manipulate and are now serving this lying spirit as their god.

The bible says the people of God are forever learning but never coming into the knowledge of the truth. The problem is, the people of God will not study God's word to show themselves approved unto God. After leaving church there are some who never open their bibles until the next Sunday in church. Study your bible, the truth shall make you free.

Leviathan the Spirit of Satan

Job 41:34, Leviathan is the king over all the sons of pride, We must guard our selves against the spirit of pride. One of the greatest spiritual warfare weapons in walking with God is humility, humbly your self to the almighty God. Foot of pride, Psalm, 36:1-11. the mouth of the foolish is a rod, Prov14:3. Crown of pride Isaiah, 28:13.Great pride. Jeremiah13:9+10, Great pride. Jeremiah13:9+10 Idolatry. Pride of life,1 John 2:15,16, causes disobedient and the love of the world.

Pride of Moab, Judah, Sodom, Israel, Philistines, Assyria. Jeremiah, 48:29, and 13:9, Ex16:49, Hosea 5:5, Zech. 9: 6, and 10:1. causes arrogance, haughtiness. Loftiness, and self exaltation. Satan uses the spirit of pride to defeat you in spiritual warfare, the weapon to defeat the spirit of pride is compassion and humility. Satan is the father of pride. You must pull down this strong hold and destroy It's power.

Demons are subject to us

Luke 10:19, Behold I give you power to tread on serpents and scorpions, and over all the power of the enemy and nothing by no mean shall hurt you, Tread mean to trample, to hit, sting, smite and strike: God has put Satan under our feet it is our Job to keep him under. Demons are subject to the power of God's word, God has given to us power over all the power of the enemy, use it. Demons are subject to the name of Jesus. we have the power to invade the enemies territory and command the enemy to leave in the name of Jesus. The spirit of darkness must be forbidden to control or harass us.

Rom. 8:14, for as many as are led by the spirit, they are the sons of God as a son of God our words has power. Mathew 17:20, you shall say to the mountain remove to yonder places and it shall remove and nothing shall be impossible to you. the next thing to do is cancel out Satan's assignments using the name of Jesus. the minute you speak the word cancel out, it is done. you shall have what you ask.

Satan The Accuser Of The Brother

Satan is the accuser of the brothers, every sin you commit Satan go to God to accuse you. His accusation will no longer work, the accuser has been cast down he is no longer in heaven. Jesus was aware of the fact that Satan would attack you in your weakness vulnerable areas, God has always been ahead of Satan, Jesus was wounded for our transgression, says if we Say we have no Sin we are a liar, if we confess our sin, God will forgive us and will cleanse us from all unrighteousness, he is faithful and just. The litter foxes destroy the vine, Satan's lie to you is, the little sins are ok, he is a lie, small or big, sin is sin. Repent daily and each night before going to bed. Stay ready for the coming of the Lord:

If Jesus should return in the night, make sure you repented before closing your eyes. It would be a disaster to wake up in the face of the antichrist: don't miss God. Rev.12:10, 1 John 1: 8: V-10, in this the children of God is manifested and the children of the devil is manifested.

THE GOOD SEED

Matt 13: 24-30: Jesus sowed good seed in the field, the good seed represent the people of the kingdom. Matt.13: 37, he who sowed good seed is the Son of man. Verse, 38, the good seed are the children of the kingdom, we are the good seed. If you sin, repent and obey this principle, I John, Cha 3: 5, and you know that Jesus was manifested to take away our sins and in him is no sin. the word of God declare whoever is born of God doth not commit sin for God's seed remains in you, you will not be able to continue in sin because you are truly born of God had planted in you his seed of righteousness which has been in our hearts. his love bring us into repentance he will not allow you to remain in sin.

David sinned but because God's seed had been planted in him, God's conviction led him to repentance Psalm Cha.51, wash me thoroughly from my iniquity and cleanse me from my sins. For I acknowledge my transgressions and my sin is ever before me. He said purge me with hyssop and I shall be whiter than snow, he ask God to create in him a clean heart and renew with in him a right spirit. David obeyed the principles of God, repentance. The bible said God heard him and delivered him out of all his fears.

Heb. 12: 6, for whom the Lord love he chasten and scourge every son whom he receives. If you endure chastening, God deal with you as sons. Jesus said all those the father has given me no man is able to pluck them out of my hands. God has declared us righteous. The good seed has been chosen before the foundation of the world, and are sitting in heavenly places with Christ Jesus.1 John 2:24, let therefore abide in you that which you heard from the beginning, in doing this, you shall stand. And when you have done all to stand, keep on standing, when your knees get weak God will carry you, strengthen you and put you back on your feet.

The good and Bad Seed

The bad seed are the children of Satan, The difference between the good seed and the bad seed, V-10, in this the children of God is manifested and the children of the devil is manifested. While men slept his enemy came and sowed tares among the wheat and went his way, and when the blade was sprung up and brought fruit then appeared the tares also, the servant asked? Did not you sow good seed in the field? How did the tare get here? Jesus said an enemy done this. The servant said should we go and gather them up? Jesus said no, lest while you gather up the tares you root also the wheat with them, let both grow together until the harvest in the time of harvest I will say to the reapers gather ye together first the tares and bind them in bundles to burn them but gather the wheat into my barn. The bad seed are planted by the devil, the tares are the children of the wicked one. He who does not righteousness is not of God, neither is he that love not his brother, these are the children of the devil manifested, they continue to sin without repentance, they have no change of heart.

GOD COVENANT BLESSINGS

We have inherit the blessings of God, they are our, believe and receive them. God speaks in his word, what does it profit a man to gain the whole world and lose his soul, Jesus said I came that you might have life and have it more abundantly. Deuteronomy 28 Cha. The covenant blessings are ours and are based on our obedience. it is written, if you are willing and obedient you shall eat the good of the land, you shall eat in plenty and shall bless the name of the Lord.

Prosperity for God's people

I wish above all things that thou may prosper and be in health and prosper as thou soul proper. God consider prosperity, to prosper God's way doing righteously. Book of Jeremiah, God said, I know the plans that I have planned for you to do you good and not evil that you might have a hope and a good future. Psalm 35:27, God has pleasure in the prosperity of his servant. The world call material gain prosperity, the meaning for prosperity for the people of God is found in DEU. Cha.28:1-14, blessings for obedience fret not thyself because of him who prosper in his own way, who bring wicked devices to pass, Ps. 37: 7 because of the man who say our prosperity is Gods covenant blessing. Psalm 1:22, they shall prosper that love thee. God promised Abraham he would bless him and his seed after him. we are the seed of Abraham.

God had no one to swear by he swore by himself he would bless us. God will not break his law. Fret not thy self of evil doers, neither be envious against the workers of iniquity, they shall soon be cut off and wither as the green herb. The curses are to the disobedient, the blessings are to the obedient, The covenant blessing are based on obedient, it is the long way, but the safe way, others are blessing themselves at any cost. What profit a man to gain the world and lose his soul. The soul that sin it shall die, there are descent people who do not know God but are prospering, but if they have not been born again, at the time of the rapture their souls will be lost, all those who have strived to gain material things and rejected Christ will be left behind, and if they die without Christ, their soul will be lost and all their gain will be left behind.

The disobedient are the fearful and the unbelieving, the abominable, the murderer, the whoremonger, the sorcerers, the idolaters and all liars shall have their part in the lake of fire, this group continues in sin, Revelation 12 chapter. God is encouraging the believers to trust in the Lord and do good so shall you dwell in the land, and thy shall be fed, delight also thyself in the Lord and he shall give thee the desires of thy heart, commit thy way unto the Lord, trust also in him and he shall bring it to pass, Ps 37.

And he shall bring forth thy obedience as the light. rest in the Lord and wait patiently for him, fret not your self because of him who prosper in his way because of the man who bring wicked devices to pass, for evildoers shall be cut off. Don't get upset when you see the world prospering in riches and wealth beautiful homes and fancy cars, it does not mean they are blessed of God. Psalm 37: 22, for such as be blessed of him shall inherit the earth; And they that be cursed him shall be cut off.

Be Strong And Stand

Ephesians Cha.6: God commands you to be strong in the Lord and in the power of his might. without God we are helpless and powerless God is the source of our strength, our power comes from God, he has given to you a spiritual amour to wear and spiritual weapons for your protection to fight against the enemy, Ephesians Cha, 6, For we wrestle not against flesh and blood but principalities, powers the rulers of darkness of this world, spiritual wickedness in high places, wherefore take unto you the whole army of God that you may be able to stand against the wiles of the devil.

having done all to stand, stand, stand therefore having your lions girt about with truth believing, trusting, and holding on until your hope is manifested. during the season of your testing do not retreat, it is important that you stay at your assigned post, don't leave the battle ground. endurance will help you to stand and go though the battle. Your adversary the devil has already been defeated. Some one asked a question? if Satan has been defeated why do we fight this warfare battle? God has given us an assignment to work out our soul salvation.

The Strength Of Ester

the glory of God was seen upon Ester, God brought her to the king. her strength was her victory, she was strong in the Lord and in the power of his might. Ester had no ideal her future had been preordained by God. Her destiny was to become queen, as she was being prepared to go before the king, her faith was strong, her integrity was her strength, her wisdom was her teacher and the favor of God was her encouragement. the office of Vas-Ti as Queen was temporarily, she was exit out and Ester was escorted into her divine destiny. She could not be stopped. God's word said, I will work and who shall let it, God had planned her destiny before the foundation of the would.

Patience Seed Timing+ Harvest

The word is planted which brings forth the seed of faith, faith causing you to hold on to patience until the appointed time for your harvest. you must go though with an attitude of expectation to receive. It is necessary that you carry with you your shield of faith which will quench all the fiery dots of the enemies of doubt. During this season your dress code depends on your victory, your victory depends on your attitude in waiting. Having your lions girt about with truth, the word of God, believing in faith nothing doubting. You must have on the breast plate of righteousness and your feet shod with the preperation of the gospel of peace, the helmet of salvation the covering for your head covered.

While Waiting On Your Harvest

* every imagination must be cast down
* every captivity must be bought under your feet
* every strong hold must be pulled down

* your communication line to God open
* always praise, worship and thanksgiving
* show God appreciation
* Gratitude for his goodness.

Psalm 92, It is good to say thanks to the Lord and to sing praises unto him. the God who is above all gods, Every morning tell him thank you for his kindness and every evening rejoice in his faithfulness sing his praises, you have done so much for me, o Lord, no wonder I am glad! I sing for joy.

O lord, what miracles you do! Psalm 95, Come before him with thankful hearts, come kneel before the Lord our maker, for he is God, We are his sheep and he is our Shepherd, sing out his praises! Bless his name.

Psalm 104, I bless the Lord: O Lord my God, how great you are!

Psalm106, Hallelujah! Thank you, Lord! How good you are! Your love for us continues on forever

Psalm 107, Thank you for being so good and kind.

GOD EXAMPLE OF PRAYER

Prayer gives confidence, adoration, thanksgiving, petition, intercession, supplication in the spirit. Jesus tells us in Matt 6: 5-14, but when you pray use not vain repetitions as the heathen do for they think they should be heard for their much speaking. Prayer is to be done to God and not to man. Jesus is not condemning public prayer but the misuse of it. God said, do not sound a trumpet before thee, as the hypocrites do in the synagogues and in the street, that they may be heard of men, they have their reward, but when you pray enter into thy closet, [the sincerity of your heart] and shut the door, pray to thy father which is in secret and thy father will see in secret and shall reward you openly but when you pray use not vain repetitions, as the heathen. Pray sincerely from your heart, God look at the heart, it is impossible to manipulate God, he know what is in the heart, he is a spirit he searches the heart. The heart is wicked above all thing who shall know only God.

The believer should not make a show of his prayer in such a way as to call attention unto himself. Jesus condemns this kind of prayer. Verse 7, the length of prayer does not move God, but the strength of the prayer that prevails with God, he is not condemning lengthy prayers, he is emphasizing that prayer, your prayer must be sincere expression. God is not impressed with words, but genuine outcry of a needy heart. Verse 8, your father know what you have need of before you ask.

The Lord's Prayer

Verse 9, after this matter pray ye: Our father which are in heaven, Hallowed be thy name; reverence to God's name and his person:

to be held in reverence and awe of holiness the sacred of his name.

This prayer is directed to our heavenly father, only a child of God who has been born again can rightly pray this prayer.

Thy kingdom come; Refers to the nature of the prayer, the kingdom is to be prayed for because it has not yet arrived.

The kingdom represents the full and effective reign of God, the effective rule of God on earth, when the last enemy. Sin and death has been destroyed at the Lord's return.

Thy will be done in earth as it is in heaven, emphasizes the ideal that prayer is to bring about conformity of the will of the believers to the will of God.

Prayer is an expression which bring us into conformity to the nature and the will of God.

Give us this day our daily bread, apply to the provision of food in general, and spiritual food.

Forgive us our debts, as we forgive our debtors, referring to sin which are our moral and spiritual debt to God's righteousness, the request of the forgiveness of sin is made for the believer for continuing spiritual growth and cleansing. the believer must acknowledge his sins, we are confessing we are sinners saved by grace, the same as we ask God to forgive us we must forgive others.

Lead us not into temptation, A plea for the providential help of God in our daily confrontation with the temptation of sin. James 1: 13, makes it clear that God does not tempt us to do evil, but rather we are tempted of our own lust God test us in order to give us the opportunity to prove our faithfulness to him. Is never his desire to lead us into evil itself, therefore if we resist the devil we are promised that he will flee from us.

Deliver us from evil. deliver from the evil that is with in us The prayer closes with a praise, for thine is the kingdom and the power and the glory forever Amen.

In the first three petitions of the prayer of the Lord, our soul rises directly to God. In the three following we face the hindrances of these aspirations and in the last petition we discover the solution to all these different ficulties. In the first petition the believers soul is awed with the character of God, in the second petition with his grand purpose, and in the third petition with his moral condition. In the second part of the prayer the children of God humble themselves independence upon divine mercy, in the fourth petition they seek forgiveness In the fifth petition gracious guidance. The Six petition the deliverance from the power of evil.

The word of God said Make your request known unto the Lord in prayer

Long suffering and thanks giving. The prayers of the righteous availed much God said his ears are open unto the righteous and he hear their cry.

Relationship with God

Hallowed be thy name
Thy Kingdom come
Thy will be done Hallowed.

Beatitudes:

Blessed are the poor in spirit for theirs is the kingdom o heaven

The Lord's prayer:

Hallowed be thy name (the name of God which opens to us the kingdom of heaven

Thy Kingdom come (heavenly comfort into our hearts

The Lord's prayer: Thy kingdom come (heavenly comfort into our hearts

Beatitude. Blessed are the meek for they shall inherit the earth

The Lord's Prayer. Thy will be done on earth as it is in heaven. the characteristic of heaven, shall posses the new earth)

Beatitude. Blessed are they that hungry and thirst after righteousness for they shall be filled

The Lord's Prayer. Give us this day our daily bread

Beatitude. Blessed are the merciful for they shall obtain mercy.

The Lord's Prayer. For give us our debts as we for give our debtors

Beatitude. Blessed are the pure in heart for they shall see God

The Lord's Prayer. And lead us not into temptation

Blessed Are The Peacemaker. God delivers us from evil

God's relationship to men
Give us this day our daily bread
Forgive us our debt
Lead us not into temptation
Deliver from evil.

Finally the doxology expresses the certain hope that our prayers shall be heard and that God in view of his great character will bring to pass the highest good in our lives Thus, prayer is the expression of the believer's confidence in the ultimate plan and purpose of God.

Guard Your Post

keep from harm, watch over, protect, defend and shield. It is a position of defense. Before the devil attack, a good guard will be alert to watch out for attack. When the guard sees or hear trouble he or she immediately protects with the shield of faith you stop the enemies attack.

The Girdle Of Truth

Truth is when we speak clearly and honestly. Proverbs 8: 6,7 hear for I will speak of excellent things and the opening of my lips shall be right things for my mouth shall speak truth and wickedness is an abomination to my lips. Proverbs 16: 6,7, by mercy and truth iniquity is purged and by the fear of the Lord, men depart from evil. We do spiritual warfare on a daily basis just by walking in mercy and truth.

Ephesians cha. 6, Shod your feet with the preparation of the gospel of peace. The opposite of peace is turmoil and confusion.

Psalm 37: 23, the steps of a good man are order by the Lord

Psalm119:105,Thy word is a lamp unto my feet and a Light unto my path.

Psalm 23, He make me to lie down in green pastures he lead me beside the still waters he restore my soul he lead me in the path of righteousness for his name sake, Yea though I walk through the valley of the shadow of death I will fear no evil for thou are with me, the word peace is translated in the greet as prosperity, quietness, and rest in times of distress and give to us quietness and rest.

Beware! Satan brings confusion and distress in the valley. Luke 1:79, God gives us light as we are walking in the shadow of death Psalm 56:13, for thou hast delivered my soul from death, will not thy deliver my feet from falling that I may walk before God in the light of the living.

Inner Armor

Put on your inner armor

* kindness
* compassion
* humility
* gentleness
* patience.

while wearing this inner protection, God is building your character, he is also teaching you how to respond to God and others in a Godly matter.

Stop fighting among your selves:

James 4:1-3, From whence come wars and fighting among you? even of your lust that war in your members, ye lust and have not, you kill and desire to have and cannot obtain you fight and war, yet you have not because you ask amiss, that you may consume it upon your lust, lust translated in the Greek, a longing for what is forbidden, a desire to covert, to set the heart upon, wanting something that does not belong to you. Setting your heart on something with a wrong motive. If this is to you, don't deny the truth, admit it, repent and ask God for deliverance, he will forgive you and cleanse you from all unrighteousness.

RECOGNIZE THE ATTACK
OF THE ENEMY

Beware of Satan's attack. His purpose is to destroy the unity. We will not allow him to divides the body of Christ we must come together in unity as a mighty army and fight. It is written where there is unity there is strength. We must protect our body. We are watchman for each other as soon as the enemy is recognized among the body we will pull it down with prayer and fasting. The anointing destroys the yoke. In the name of Jesus we pray for our sister and brother for deliverance from Jealousy and envy and strife. God has commanded us to love one each other, love destroys the attacks of the enemy

Help against Our Enemies

When our enemies attack us, Psalm 18: The Lord is my fort where I can enter and be safe no one can follow me in and slay me, he is a rugged mountain where I can hide, he is my savior, a rock where none can reach me, and a tower of safety he is like the strong horn of a mighty fighting bull all I need to do is cry to him Oh praise the Lord and I am saved from all my enemies! Death bound me with chains and the flood s of ungodliness mounted a massive attack against me, trapped and helpless, I struggled against the ropes that drew me on to death. In my distress I screamed to the Lord for help, and he heard me from heaven, then the earth rocked and reeled, and the mountain shook and tremble, how they quaked!

Save me, O Lord, by your name sake and vindicate me by your strength, hear my prayer, O Lord give ear to the words of my mouth for strangers have risen up against me and oppressors have sought after my life.

God's Anger

[Touch not my anointed and do my prophets no harm]

Fierce flames leaped from his mouth, setting fire to the earth, smoke blew from his nostrils. He bent the heavens down and came to my defense, thick darkness was beneath feet, Mounted on the cherubim, he sped swiftly to my aid with wings of wind. He enthroned himself with darkness, veiling his approach with dense clouds as murky waters, suddenly the brilliance of his presence broke through the cloud with lightning and a mighty storm of hail.

Haters OF God's People

the tares, the angels of light, Satan ministers the counterfeit prophets, the Jezebel spirits, the Shiite spirits, the Shiite are descended of Abraham, his first son Ishmael, hated Isaac because he was the promised son until this day the descendent of Ishmael hate the chosen people of God, and those who reject God, hate you. don't allow Satan to run you out of house of God. Many of the saints have backslid for that reason, we are to assemble our selves together with the people of God: fellowship Is important among the saints. You must remember we are the church, the house of God is a place the saints gather to worship God.

The house of God is a place for sinners gather to find Jesus and for backsliders return back to God—and a place for saints to receive encouragement and strength from one another. those who reject Christ, the haters will always be present in the house of God.

People attend church for different reasons, every body is not in church for God. The truth is, the body of Christ is the true church. Jesus said, by love all men shall know you are my disciples. God has warned his body to watch as well as pray; the reason is because your adversary is out to destroy. God is our help The Lord thundered in the heaven. the God above all Gods has spoken, Oh, the hail, the hailstones, oh the fire! He flashed his fearful arrows of lightning and routed, all my enemies, see how they run.

he reached down from heaven and took me and drew me out of my great trial. And rescued me from deep waters, He delivered me from my strong enemy, from those who hated me, I was helpless in their hands.

Psalm 7, we cry unto God as David cried out, I am depending on you, O Lord my God, to save me from my persecutors. don't let them pounce upon me as a lion would and maul me and drag me away with no one to rescue me, arise in anger against the anger of my enemies awake! demand justice for me.

Psalms 31, We cry as David cried out, pull me from the trap my enemies have set for me, for you alone is strong enough.

1 Peter 4:14, If ye be reproached for the name of Christ, happy are you, for the spirit of glory and of God rest upon you on their part he is evil spoken of, but on your part he is glorified.

1 Peter 4:14, But rejoice, as much as ye are partakers of Christ sufferings that, when his glory shall be revealed, ye may be glad also. Ps. 19:1, The heavens declare the glory of God and the firmament showed his handiwork. Ps 16: 9+10, Therefore my heart is glad and my glory rejoice, my flesh also shall rest in hope for thy will not leave my soul in hell neither will thou suffer thy Holy one to see corruption. (For this you should give God glory.

Palms 35, O Lord, fight those fighting me, declare war on them for their attack on me, put on your armor, take your shield and protect me by standing in front, lift your spear in my defense for my pursuers are getting very close, let me hear you say you will save me from them, dishonor those who are trying to kill me, turn them back and confuse them, I will rejoice in the Lord, he shall rescue me, who else protects the weak from those who would rob them.

SATAN ATTACTS	GOD'S WEAPON
Spirit of bondage	spirit of adoption, freedom. And liberty
Spirit fear	spirit of power, love, and a sound mind
Deaf and dumb spirit	God's life, truth, Gifts of healing and miracles
Spirit of heaviness	God's garments of praise, oil of joy, comfort
Spirit of infirmity	God's life, healing and miracles
Spirit of jealousy	God's love, compassion, generosity
Perverse spirit	Good and excellent spirit the spirit of truth
Spirit of divination	Accuracy in the Gifts of the Spirit Truth
Spirit of whoredom	God's love
Spirit of haughtiness	Humble and contrite spirit
Lying spirit	God's truth
Antichrist spirit	Truth and Love
Unclean spirit	Clean Spirit
Spirit of err and religion	truth and righteousness
seduction spirit	truth
Love of money	Generosity and wisdom
Violence, fear	Love
jealousy	Love
Rebellious spirit	God's power, love and a sound
Death and fear	Spirit of life in Christ

According to the word of God I pray that the eyes of your understanding would be enlightened before going into battle your flesh must be discipline and submit to the Holy Sprit: The Holy Spirit will produce in you the fruit of the spirit. Gal 5: 22-26, love, joy, peace, longsuffering, gentleness, goodness, faith meekness, temperance.

Adultery

Having relationship with someone else other than your husband or your wife, resist Satan and he will flee, otherwise you will be excluded from the battle

Fornication

Single Christians having sex relation without marriage

Resist Satan and he will flee, otherwise you will be excluded from the battle

Uncleanness

Touch not the unclean thing and I will receive you

Resist Satan and he will flee, otherwise you will be excluded from the battle.

Lascivious

Unruly. Out of order, disobedient, unchaste

Resents God's chastisement: do not resist chastisement, God chase those whom he love other wise you are considered as a bastard.

Idolatry serving another god, other than the true God continuing to serve without repentance, in the day of Judgment God will say to you, depart from me I never knew I never knew you.

Witchcraft control, controlling the minds of others

Control. Controlling minds of others, it is not God's will that any should perish but that all come to repentance.

Hatred hating instead of loving, how can you say you love God and hate your brother whom you see everyday God said the love of God is not in you.

Emulation eagle or ambitious to equal or excel another competitors, this is vain, to enter into the kingdom of heaven is to follow the plain of God.

Wrath anger, this is a spirit from Satan it brings you into the area of harming others, resist Satan and he will flee.

Strife bitter, violent, conflict fight, struggle.

Sedition incitement of resistance to or of insurrection against lawful authority, God commands you to be wise in all things.

Heresy middle voice caring news, one who does this is totally going against the will of God, stay out of matters that does not concern you, otherwise you are a busy body and God will deal with you.

Envying painful or resentment awareness of an advantage enjoyed by another joined with a desire to posses the same advantage. This is a spirit from Satan, it brings with it jealousy the bible say jealousy is as cruel as the grave.

Murder to spoil by performing in a wretched manner. this is a spirit from Satan, you can murder an individual by attacking his or her character.

Drunken unsteady or lurking as if from intoxication.

Rebelling opposition to one in authority Hebrew 13:17, obey them who have ruler over you, they watch over your soul, as they that must give account, that that may do it with joy, and not with grief for that is unprofitable for you. Paul said, follow me as I follow Christ, follow after righteousness and holiness. Roman 14:19, let us follow those things which make for peace and things that edify one another those who does not edify your soul flee from them.

Works Of The Holy Spirit

* Luke 12:12, the holy spirit is a teacher.
* John 12: 26, a comforter.
* Act 2: 38, a gift.
* Roman 14:17, the Holy Spirit gives to you joy and peace.
* Ephesians 1:22, the Holy Spirit presents you holy and blameless.
* The Holy Spirit is the keeper of your soul if you desire.
* The Holy Spirit is a guide, Ps. 31: 3, David said lead and guide me.
* Ps. 32: 8, the Holy Spirit will guide you with his eyes.
* John 16:13, the Holy Spirit will guide you into all truth.
* Jude 2: 24, the Holy Spirit will keep you from falling.
* Proverb 11: 3,The Holy Spirit will guide the upright.
* Proverb 23: 19, the Holy Spirit guide your heart in the ways of God.

Fruits of the holy spirit

Galatians 5: 22

God produces these fruits in the lives of the surrendered Christian.

* **Love** yourself, your neioborhood and God.
* **Joy** in the time of trouble and despair.
* **Peace** he open your heart to receive it.
* **long suffering** he give you his grace to go though suffering.
* **Patience** he opens your heart to receive patience in waiting.
* **kindness** he opens your heart to be kind to others.
* **goodness** he opens your heart to do good things.
* **faithfulness** he causes you to be faithful to him and to others.
* **gentleness** he opens your heart to be gentle to others.
* **self control** he gives us self control in waiting and making decisions.
* **endurance** he gives us his endurance power to endure pain of suffering.

Endurance

During your season of testing you must carry with you endurance, this fruit work with patience. Patience from a Latin word mean to suffer. Patience challenge a child of God to wait in the midst of suffering or to endure some tribulation without complaint. To grow in patience, a child of God must bear pain or trouble without losing self control or becoming disturbance to others. In portraying this quality, a child of God calmly tolerates delay while refusing to be provoked by it.

Mark 13:13, he who shall endure unto the end shall be saved, saved from your doubts and fear and from the destruction of Satan,

2 Timothy 2: 3, therefore endured hardness as a good soldier of Jesus Christ.

The Sewer Went Forth To Sow

Matt. Cha13:4, a sewer went forth to sow, and when he sowed some seed fell by the way side, some fell upon stony places, some fell among throne, others fell among good ground he that received seed in stony places hear the word and anon which received it he had no root in himself, endured for a while when tribulation or persecution come because of the word by and by he is offended.

He is not able to endure. those who fell among stony places, heard the word but did not open their heart to receive seed, because they refuse to give up the world and the cares of the world, some has become church members but not true believers, those who received the word among thorns, hear the word but because of deceitfulness of riches, choked the word and became unfruitful.

Leaders, church members which ever group fit you, I pray for your deliverance, in the name of Jesus: John Cha. 3:3-7 the word of God declare, you must be born again, baptized in the water and in the Holy Spirit other wise you cannot enter into the kingdom of God. Those with out the holy spirit does not have the spirit of God; their lives are absent from the anointing: unless they repent and receive Jesus, they are headed for destruction.

Mega churches, large membership, big find houses, beautiful cars, millions of dollars diamonds nor pearl, none of these things impresses God, the one thing that impresses God is your sacrifice of obedience: Matt 15:8, the people draw nigh unto me with their mouth but their heart is far from me, in vain do they worship me teaching for doctrine the commandments of man.

Why say Lord, Lord, and do not the things I say. Unless the Lord build a house the laborer labor in vain.

Know them by their fruit

Matt 7:20, You shall know them by their fruit, a corrupt tree brings forth evil fruit and cannot bring good fruit. Every tree that bring not forth good fruit is hewn down and is cast into the fire. Any one who fail to abide in the vine will wither and dry up; anything that withers has no life: the Holy Spirit only can gives life. A good tree bring forth good fruit, it is impossible for it to bring forth bad fruit; and impossible for a corruptible tree to bring forth good fruit: you shall know then by their fruit.

The Benefit to them Who Abide In The Vine

John 15: 7, if you abide in the vine, and my words abides in you, you shall ask what ever you will and it shall be done unto you. Jesus said to them, the time will come when I shall no more speak to you in proverb but I shall show you plainly of the father. henceforth I call you not servants but I call you friends, for all things that I have heard of my father I have made it known unto you.

And I will say unto you, that I will pray the father for you. from the Tyndale bible, Jesus said, Then you will present your petition over my signature. And I wont need to ask the father to grant you these request, for the father himself love you dearly, because you love me, and believe that I came from the father.1 John 5:14, And this is the confidence that we have in him, that, if we ask anything according to his will, he hear us. And if we know that he hear us, whatsoever we ask. We know that we have the petition that we desire of him.

Here, we see God was four days late but on time, your prayer will be answered on God's time clock, you shall see the glory of God. John 11:40-43, Lazarus was dead four days and stinking Jesus said. Mary If thou would believe, thou shall see the glory of God, Verse 42+ 42, Jesus prayed the answer, father I thank thee for the answer, father I thank thee thou hast heard me and I know that thy hear me always. Verse 43, Jesus called those thing that was not as thou they were, Jesus called the answer forth and Lazarus come forth. We are to do the same, call things that be not and watch them come forth.

John 5: 14, Jesus said, I say unto you, The Son can do nothing of himself but what he see the father do, for whatsoever he do, these also do the Son do likewise. Jesus remembered his father's words in Gen. Cha.1:3, And God said let their be light and there were Light, God spoke the word into existence and light came forth. Jesus spoke the word into existence and Lazarus came forth. Jesus did the same as he saw his father do. We have the same power God expect us to do the same.

Mark 11: 23, he shall have what ever he say. Verse 24, whatsoever things ye desire when you pray believe you receive them and ye shall have them.

GOD'S GLORY

God's Glory is worship, praise honor and thanksgiving, to rejoice proudly.

Matt.6: 13, For thine is the kingdom the power and the glory forever amen: Ps. 24: 7-10, life up your heads o ye gates and be lifted up, ye ever lasting doors. And the king of glory shall come in who is the king of glory? The Lord strong and mighty in battle.2 Thessalonians 2:12, We are called to his glory, chosen before the foundation of the world. 1 Peter, 1: 3, he has called us to glory

And virtue, Virtue meaning, courage, moral action or excellence, Chastity,

The virtue of accepting correction graciously. Ephesians 3: 16, that he would grant you according to his riches s glory, to be strengthen with might by his spirit in the inner man.

1 Peter 1:8, Whom having not seen, you love, in whom though now ye see him not, yet believing, you rejoice with joy unspeakable and full of glory. Ps 64: 10, the righteous shall be glad in the Lord and shall trust in Him and all the upright in heart shall glory.

Ephesians 5: 23, For the husband is the head of the wife even as Christ is the head of the church. and he is the Savior of the body. That he might present it to himself a glorious church.

Ps. 93: 3, Declare his glory among the heathen, his wonders among all the people. Roman 4: 20, Abraham straggled not at the promise of God though unbelief but was strong in faith giving glory to God.

Roman 8: 17+18, We are children and heirs of God and joint heirs with Christ. if so be that we suffer with Christ, that we may be also glorified together. For I reckon that the suffering of this present time are not worthy to be compared with the glory which shall be revealed in us.

1 Corinthians 11:7, The man is the image and glory of God, The woman is the glory of the man, a woman hair is her glory. Jeremiah 9: 23, Thus said the Lord let not the wise man glory in his wisdom neither the mighty man glory in his might, let not the rich man glory in his riches but he that glories let him glory in the Lord. John 13: 31+32, Jesus said, now is the Son of man glorified and God is glorified in him. If God be glorified in him, God shall also glorify, him in himself: John 15: 8, Herein is my father glorified that ye bear much fruit: so shall ye be my disciples. who being the brightness of his glory the express image of his person.

John 17: 4, I have glorified thee on the earth, I have finished the work you have given me to do. Colossians 3: 4, when Christ who is our life shall appear, we shall appear with him in his glory. Hebrew 1: 2+3, He made the worlds, with him in his glory.

THESE SHALL NOT ENTER INTO THE KINGDOM OF HEAVEN

Matt 7: 21, Jesus said not every one that says Lord shall enter into the kingdom heaven, the defiled shall not enter into the kingdom of heaven. Many will say in that day Lord have we not prophesied in thy name? and in thy name done wonderful works? And in thy name we cast out devils? And in thy name done wonderful works? And then I will confess before my father I never know you depart, from me you worker of iniquity.

Mark 7:20, Jesus said that which come out of the man, that defile the man, from within out of the heart of men, proceeded evil fornication, murder, thefts, covetousness, wickedness, deceit, lasciviousness, an evil eye, blasphemy, pride, foolishness, wanting that which belong to others, envy, slander pride, all these things comes from with in and defile the man and all other folly, these things pollute the person and make them unfits for God to use in his kingdom.

John 15:2, I am the true vine every branch in me that bring not fruit he takes away. verse 6: If a man abided not in me, he is cast into the fire and is burned and if he abides not in me he is cast forth as a branch and is withered and men gather them and cast them in the fire and they are burn. If you abide in me and I abide in you, you will ask what you will and it shall be done unto you.

This book is written to enlightens your eyes to the knowledge of God's truth and to give you a sense of your identity of who you are and the power you posses over your enemies

Milk and Meat

Hebrew 4:12, for when the time you ought to be teachers

You have need that one teach you again which be the first principle of the oracles of God, and are become such as have need of milk, and not of strong meat. forevery one who uses milk is unskillful in the word of righteousness for he is a babe, but strong meat belonged to them that are of full age, even those who by reason of use have their senses exercised to discern both good and evil. We fall down but we get up, it is time for you to come out of carnality, give up your fleshly desires. a carnal minded man cannot please God, this is the time for you to get up and stand up for Christ, God' purpose for you is to move you from a baby into maturity.

Repentance

1 John 1:9 if we say that we have no sin, we deceive ourselves and the truth is not in us. face your dark side, do not deny it, confess it God promised to forgive our sins and cleanse us from the unrighteousness. Rev 2: 5, remember where you have fallen and repent, and do the first work or else I will come upon you quickly and will remove thy candlestick out of his place except thy repent:

Rev. 3:3, remember how you have received and heard, hold fast and repent. If therefore thy shall not watch, I will come upon you like a thief and you shall not know what hour I will come up on you, Rev, 3: 15+ 16, I know thy works that thy are neither cold nor hot, I would that thy was cold or hot, because you are lukewarm I will spit thee out of my mouth. Rev. 22: 14+15, bless are they who do his commandments, that they may have the right to the tree of life that they may enter in though the gates into the city. **Rev 22: 16,** these shall not enter, dogs, sorcerers and whoremongers and murderers, and idolaters, and whoever love and make a lie.

THE RIGHTEOUSNESS
OF GOD REVEALED

Roman I:17-32, For there is the righteousness of God revealed from faith to faith. for the wrath of God is revealed from heaven against all ungodliness and unrighteousness of men, who hold the truth in unrighteousness, because that which might be known of God is manifest in them, for God hath shown it to them. For the invisible things of him from the creation of the world are clearly seen, being understood by the things that are made, even his eternal power and Godhead.

So they are without excuse, because that, when they knew God they glorified him not as God, neither were thankful. but became vain in their imagination and their hearts were darkened. Professing to be wise they became fools, wherefore God gave them up to uncleanness though the lust of their own hearts, to dishonor their own bodies between themselves who changed the truth into a lie and worshiped and served the creature more than the creator, who is blessed forever A-men.

For this cause God gave then up to vile affections. for even their women did change the nature use into that which is against nature. And likewise also the men leaving the natural use of the woman, burned in their lust one to another, men with men working that which is unseemly, and receiving in themselves that of their pay error which was meet.

And even as they did not like to retain God in their knowledge, God gave then up to a reprobate mind, to do those things that are not convenient, being filled with all unrighteousness, fornication, wickedness, covetousness, maliciousness, full of murder, debate, deceit, malignity, whisperers, backbiting, haters, of God, despiteful, proud, boasters, inventors of evil things, disobedient to parent, without understanding, covenant breakers, without natural affections, implacable, unmerciful, who knowing the judgment of God that they that commit such things are worthy of death, not only do the same but have pleasure in those that do them.

Roman 2:8+9, God says, let God be the truth and let every man be a lie. but unto them who are contentious and do not obey the truth, but obey unrighteousness, indignation and wrath. tribulation and anguish upon every soul of man that doeth evil, Roman verse 11, there is no respect of person with God. To those of you who love righteousness, Roman 2:7, but to them that are continuance in well doing seek for glory and honor and immortality eternal life.

Roman 2:10, glory honor and peace to every man that work good, to the Jews and also to the gentiles. Revelation 2:7, he that has an ear let him hear what the spirit say unto the churches. We are the church and the body of Christ. Roman 2:16, in the day God shall judge the secret of men by Jesus Christ according to my gospel. Matthew, 5:8, blessed are the pure in heart for the shall see God. People of God you are commanded to pray always and never faint, pray for God to give you a clean heart, the bible said, the heart is wicked above all things who shall know it, since we do not know the wickedness in our heart, we should constantly cry out to God.

God is coming back looking for a clean and Pure heart, clean mind and a right motive. We need to say Lord work on me. because the coming of the Lord is very near, I advise you to constantly say Lord work on me. I also advise you, to repent each day, anything you do displeasing to God, don't hesitate to repent Wisdom is to repent. You do not know the day nor the hour when the Son of man shall come, be ready at all times. Ask God to strengthen you in all your weak areas. If you do this God will prepare You for his coming. I am daily asking God to work on me.

Young Warriors

some warriors are babes but as you grow and mature God will move you into a higher position, which come not from man but from God. as you walk though the valley of the shadow of death, God is with you. resist the spirit of self righteousness. God's word declare, we all have sinned and have come short of the glory of God. All our righteousness is as filthy rags before the Lord. Remember, the small foxes destroy the vine, Satan's biggest lie is that little sin does not matter to God. Sin is sin. Jesus said to Peter, the enemy seek to sift you as wheat, but I have prayed for you that your faith fail not. Jesus has prayed for you, John 17:9.

I often hear saints say, I wonder if any one praying for me, or they say, if I ask another saint to pray for me maybe they were busy and forgot, that might be the case, if so, you should not depend on another to pray for you. Even thou Jesus have prayed for us, God has commanded us to pray for our selves. And not only to pray for our selves but to pray for all saints, we are to pray the sinners, the backsliders, our children. Our families, the world, the nation, all leaders. Those in government, the president, our young generation, our seniors. The sick, the shut in, the prisoners, our enemies, those who hate us and persecute us.

GOVERNMENT MINISTRIES

The Governmental Ministries oversee and develop these ministers in the rest of the body of Christ. Government Ministries are to prepare the saints for their various ministries. Ephesians 4:12, Perfecting the saints for the work of the ministry. These ministries help the body of Christ recognize their gifts and talent. God has chosen each one in the body of Christ to participate within the body of Christ.

The Responsibility of the government Ministries

* Adjust and repair
* Equip and train
* Place the body of Christ into the work of the ministry

Satan has planted his ministering angles within the government ministries with deception trying to oppose the plan of God and has confused the body of Christ.

Matt 13:27, the servant of the householder came and said unto him sir, did not thy sow good seed in the field? From where came the tares? He said an enemy has done this.

God's Spiritual Strategy

God gives us spiritual strategy to win the battle against the enemy He has always given strategy to his chosen people. He gave spiritual strategy to Ester, Ruth, Debra, Joshua, Gideon and Joseph; God give strategy to all of his warriors.

Trust God Wheneverything Is Going Wrong

* Money funny
* Friend few
* Enemies many
* Family problems
* Need employment
* Single and unhappy
* Too old to get married
* Too fat
* Too skinny
* Hair too short
* Nobody love me

What ever attacks he uses on you. Do not listen to Satan's foolishness, remain focus on your purpose. Delight your self in the Lord and he shall give you the desires of your heart. God declares if you keep your mind stayed on him, he shall keep you in perfect peace.

COVENANT MARRIAGE

Married is ordained by God, he put his approval on it in the garden of between Adam and Eve. he said it is not good for man to be alone, he who fineth a wife fineth a good thing. who can find a virtuous woman and who can find a faithful man? the holy spirit unites the virtuous woman and the faithful man. if you desire a husband or a wife wait on the lord. he declare in his word, whatsoever things you desire when you pray believe you receive them and you shall have them.

Eph. 5: 25-27, husbands love your wives as Christ love the Church and gave himself for it that he may sanctify it and cleanse it with the washing of the water by the word. That he might present unto himself a glorious church not having spot or wrinkle or any such thing. it should be holy and without blemish, so ought men to love their wives as their own bodies. he that love his wife love himself, for no man yet hated himself but nourishes and cherish it, even as the Lord love the church.

When you do not understand your trials in marriage, Roman 8:28 and we know that all thing work together for good to them who love God, to them who are called according to his purpose. For whom he foreknew, he did predestinated, and whom he called, them he also justified and whom he justified, them he also glorified. we are stamped and approver by God. the word of God clearly states marriage is honorable in all but the bed undefiled. God honors marriage between man and a woman, the proof is in the garden of Eden.

The first marriage was between Adam and Eve. God said in his word if you ask for bread he will not give you a stone, if you ask for a fish he will not give you a serpent. God declares, he will withhold no good thing from them who walk up right before me. those of you who desires husbands and wives wait on God, he does not make mistakes, every good and perfect gift come from the Lord And the father of light. Receiving that which is rightfully yours depends on your faith, it's already done. confess it and believe it. the next step you are to praise God for the answer. thou the vision tarry wait for it for it shall surly come to pass.

SPIRITS ATTACKING
THE BODY OF CHRIST

Resist the spirit of doubt

James 6,-8, he who doubts is like a wave of the sea driven and tossed by the wind, for let not think he will receive anything from the Lord, he is a double minded man unstable in all of his ways. It is impossible to please God without faith. Hebrew11:1 faith is The substance of things hope for and the evidence of things not see: God's word is settled in heaven and cannot be altered

Spirit Of Bondage

Roman8:15, God has not given us the spirit of bondage. The spirit of bondage includes, compulsory sin. All addiction, such as tobacco, curing, nicotine, narcotic, alcohol, greed, lust for power, money, sex desires out side of marriage, oppression, bitterness, poverty, control, domineering spirit, coveting, bruised and broken spirit, satanic captivity, subdued spirit, controlling spirit works in cooperation with the spirit of bondage

Spirit Of Fear

11 Tim. 1:7 God has not given us the spirit of fear but of love power and a sound mind, focus on the answer, it is done.

The manifestation of fear

*Timidity
*Shyness
*Convincing other

Fear causes

Death, violence, Jealous, Sickness, Stuttering, Rejection, Murder, anxious, Poverty, Worry, Judging, Criticism, Heart Attack, Strife, tension, stress, torment, nightmare, fear of death, fear of man. The enemy uses fear as a tactic to open areas of weakness in you. The spirit of fear is a major stronghold

Spirit Of Heaviness

Manifestations are rejection, hurt mourning, hopelessness, loneliness, discouragement, abnormal grief, loss of motivation, despair, self pity, lost of joy, depression

ISA 61: 3: For the spirit of heaviness, God has appointed to you that morn in Zion to give unto you beauty for ashes, the oil of joy for mourning, the garment of praise for the spirit of heaviness that you may be called trees of righteousness, the planting of the Lord that he might be glorified.

Spirit Of Infirmity

Act 28:3, feeble of body and mind, a disease, sickness. weakness, without strength, physical, mental, emotional, lack of strength and energy, virus infections, arthritis, chronic illness, condition of sickness, incurable diseases, cancer, a spirit of inheritance that can be spoken to when delivering someone from a spirit of infirmity, it has been inherited from generation to generation because the individual did not know their authority to break those powers of darkness, the enemy attacked with a root of bitterness or forgetfulness upon them.

Luke 13:11-12, says and their was a woman had a spirit of infirmity eighteen years, and was bowed together, and could not lift herself, and when Jesus saw her he called her to him, and said to her, woman thy are loose from your infirmity, God has given to you the power and the authority to loose your self and other from their infirmity, you do not have to wait for some one else to deliver you, God has given you the power to deliver your self, the key is to believe God's word

Spirit Of Jealousy

James 3:13, manifestations are :violent, murder, suicide, anger, wrath, revenge, rage, envy strife, competitiveness, confusion, and every evil work, spitefulness, coveting, cruelty, selfishness, division in church and home, hate. fear and jealousy work together spirit of strife, cause war between countries friend families, churches.

Perverse Spirit

the manifestations are: rebellion, error, hate, self lovers, foolish words, snares, deceit, sexual perversion homosexual and lesbian spirits, deception, distortion of the word, it tries to ruin reputation twist. Perverts and promotes pornography, physical and mental abuse, a perverse spirit Put everything in perverse, evil mean good and good mean evil a perverse way of thinking.

Spirit Of Divination (witchcraft) 1 SAM. 15: 23

Witchcraft mean to whisper a spell or to practice a magic. Manifestations are: drugs, souls prophecy, hypnosis, medium, chandlers, soothsayer, horoscopes, consulting the dead, witches, games involving ghost, demons, or any kind of witchcraft, Ouija, board, works with familiar spirits, occult, controlling spirits, witchcraft and controlling spirit work together these spirits seek to counterfeit the gifts of the Holy Spirit. Those of you who has been involved in divination need to denounce their past experience and repent to God and ask him to cleanse you from all unrighteousness

Spirit Of Antichrist 1 John 4:3,

Manifestations are: cultism which denies Jesus Christ is deity opposing Revelation from God, persecution, seducers, impostors suppression of ministries, this spirit causes people to seek to bring praise to themselves, they attack and try to destroy Christians, this spirit opposes Christ and all that has to do with the blood of Jesus, the spirit of error and the new age movement, one world government, is involved with this spirit of antichrist, 666, antichrist is putting things in order for his coming, God has commanded you to watch as well as pray, listen to news, watch your television, stay alert.

Spirit Of Error And Religion

1 John 4: 6, We are from God, he who know God listen to us. he who is not from God does not listen to us, by this we know the spirit of truth and the manifestations of these spirits are: religion causes strife, Jealousy, contradiction, arguing, love of money, selfish gain, abuse of God's people. The spirit of religion causes spiritual death to an individual and cause the spirit of err to work in their lives. The spirit of religion and the spirit of error work with lying spirits and cause one not to hear or speak the correct information or to see the word of God correctly. The spirit of error is the root of religion. God has commanded his church to destroy these spirits and to pull down their strong hold.

Manipulation

Those who manipulate, get others to do things for benefiting themselves rather than the one being manipulated, this spirit take away one's self motivation, pressure others and take away their choices. Satan is a good example, he manipulated Eve in the garden, persuaded her to eat the probidden fruit. Delilah manipulated Sampson, she deceived him with her beauty. He trusted her with the secret of his strength which was in his hair, she cut his hair and sold him out to the enemy, though manipulation of woman he lost everything.

Be Not Deceived

Matt.24:4, Take heed that no man deceive you, for many shall come in my name saying I am the Christ and shall deceive many.

1 Corinthians 3:18, let no man deceive himself, if any man among you seem to be wise in this world, let him become a fool, that he may be wise.

Ps. 111: 10, the fear of the Lord is the beginning of wisdom, Prov.17, the fear of the Lord is the beginning of knowledge, but fools despise wisdom and instructions. God's word are bible principles which protects you from your adversary.

1 Thessalonians 2:3, let no man deceive you by any mean, for that day shall not come except their come a falling away first, the falling away is here and that man of sin being revealed, the son of perdition, (Satan) verse7, the mystery of Iniquity do already work. Verse 8, the wicked shall be revealed. God declare, things done in the dark shall come to the light.

Ephesians 5: 6, let no man deceive you with vain words for because of these thing cometh the wrath of God upon the children of disobedience. Ephe.4:4, there is one body, and one spirit, even as you are called in the hope of your calling. John 3: 7, little children Let no man deceive you. He that doeth righteous is righteous as he is righteous. 1 John 3:8, he that commit the sin is of the devil, for the devil sinnith from the beginning. For this purpose the son of God was manifested, that he might destroy the works of the devil.

Matt. 24:22, except those days should be shorted there should be no flesh saved, but for the elect sake those days shall be shortened. Revelation 24: 24, for their shall arise false Christ,and false prophets and shall shew great signs and wonders insomuch that If it were possible they shall fool the very elect but it is not possible to fool God's elect. Amos, 3:7, Surly the Lord will do nothing, but he reveals his secret unto his servants the prophets.

Jesus is soon to return, Rev, 16: 15, Behold I come as a thief, watch therefore, for ye know not the day nor the hour where in the son of man cometh. Blessed is he that watch and keep his garment lest he walk naked, and they see his shame.

THE CHURCH WILL NOT GO THOUGH THE TRIBULATION

Rev. 3: 10, because you have kelp the word of my patience I also will keep you from the hour of temptation, which shall come upon all the world to try them that dwell on the earth. 1 Thessalonians I:10, Jesus delivered us from the wrath to come. 1 Thessalonians 5: 9, for God has not appointed us to wrath. The rapture is for the saints. Matt. 24: 13, he who endure to the end shall be saved. V-5, he that overcome the same shall we be clothes in white raiment. I will not blot out his name out of the book of life, but I will confess his name before my father and he that over come I will grant to sit with me with my father in his throne. 1 John, 5: 4+5, for whosoever is born of God overcome the victory that has overcome the world—our faith. Who is he who overcomes the word, but believers, he who believes that Jesus is the Son of God? This is he who came by water and blood—Jesus Christ not only by water, but by water and blood.

And it is the spirit who bear witness, because the Spirit is true for the three bear witness, because the Spirit is truth. For there are three that bear witness in heaven: the Father, the word and the Holy Spirit and these three are one.

And there are three that bear witness on earth: the Spirit, the water, and the blood and these three agree as one. If we receive the witness of men, the witness of God is greater; For this is the witness of God which He has testified of his Son. He who believe in the Son of God has witness in himself; and this is the testimony that God has given us eternal life, and this is in his Son.

He who has the Son has life, he who does not have the son of God does not have life I have written to you who believe in the name of The Son of God, that you may know that you have eternal life. And that you may continue to believe in the name of the Son of God.

Now this is the confidence that we have in him that, if we ask anything according to his will, He hears us. And if we know that he hears us, whatsoever we ask, we know that we have the petitions that we have asked of him.

We will be caught up in the rapture with our Lord and Savior Jesus Christ. 1Thess 4:13, but I will not have you ignorant, brethren concerning them that are sleep, that ye sorry not, even as others which has no help. For as we believe Jesus has died and rose again, even thou them which also sleep in Jesus will God bring with him. we say unto you by the word, that we which are alive and remain until the coming of the Lord shall not prevent them which are sleep. for the Lord himself shall descend from heaven which a shout with the voice of the archangel and with the trump of God and the dead shall rise first then we which are alive shall be caught up together with him in the cloud to meet him in the air, and so shall we ever be with the lord.

Great Tribulation

Matt, 24: 21, for then shall be great tribulation, such as was not since the beginning of the world until this time, no nor ever shall be. Verse 23, then if any man say unto you, lo, here is Christ, or there believe it not. For there shall arise false Christ and false prophet and shall show great signs and wonders inasmuch that, if it were possible, they shall deceive the very elect. God want you to understand it is not possible to fool his elect because he declared, I will show my secrets unto my prophets.

Jesus said unto his disciples unto you it is given to know the mystery of the kingdom of God, but unto them that are without, all things are done in parables, that seeing they may see, and not perceive; and hearing they may hear and not understand. But to you, God has given clarity to understand his mysteries; Lest at any time they should be converted, and their sins should be forgiven them. God knew from the beginning those who would reject him.

4:26, behold I have told you before wherefore if they say to you. Behold wherefore if they shall say to you behold he is in the desert go not forth behold or they say, he is in the secret chamber believe it not, for as the lighting cometh out of the east and shine even unto the west so shall also the coming of the man be. For wherever the carcase is, there will be the eagles. Mark 4:11.

The Sun Shall Be Darkened

Matthew 25: 29, immediately after the tribulation of those days shall the sun be darkened and the moon shall not give her light, and the stars shall fall from from heaven, and the powers of the heavens shall be shaken. verse 30, and then shall appear the Son of man in heaven and then all of the tribes of the earth mourn, and they shall see the Son of man coming in the clouds of heaven with power and great glory. He shall send his angels with a great sound of a trumpet, and they shall gather together his elect from the four winds, from one end of heaven to the other. V-35, heaven and earth pass away but my words shall never pass away. But of that day and hour knoweth no man, no not the angels of heaven, but my father only. watch therefore for you know not what hour your Lord cometh. Therefore be ye also ready for in such as hour that ye think not the Son of man cometh. Verse 46, blesseth is that servant, whom his Lord when he cometh shall find him so doing.

The Two Beast

Revelation 13, John saw the beast and one of his heads was wounded to death, the deadly wounds were healed all the world wondered after the beast and they worshiped the (dragon) which is Satan) which gave power the beast, they worshiped the beast saying, who is like unto the beast? Who is able to make war with him. All that dwell upon the earth shall worship him, whose names is not written in the book of life of the lamb slain before the foundation of the world. V-13, he doeth great wonders, so that he maketh fire come down from heaven on the earth in the sight of men. and deceived them that dwell on the earth by the means of those miracles which he has power to do in the sight of the beast; saying to those who dwell on the earth, that they should make an image to the beast, which had the wound by the sword and did live.

V-15, and he had power to give life unto the image of the beast should both speak, and cause that as many as would not worship the image of the beast should be killed, and he caused all both small and great, rich and poor, free and bond to receive the mark in there right hand or in their foreheads. Verse 17, and that no man shall buy or sell unless he has the mark 666 or the name of the beast.

Rev. 14: 9, and the third angle followed them, saying with a loud voice, if any man worship the beast and his image, and receive the mark on his forehead, or in his hand, the same drink of the wine of the wrath of God which is poured out without mixture into the cup of indignation and he shall be tormented with fire and brimstone in the presence of the holy angles, and in the presence of the Lamb. Verse11, and the smoke of their torment ascended up forever and ever and they have no rest day nor night, who worship the beast and his image, and whoever receive the mark of his name

THE SEALS ARE OPENED

Revelation Cha. 5, John said, I saw in the right hand of him that sit on the throne a book written in and on the backside, sealed with seven seals. when the lamb opened **one of the seals** the noise was as thunder, John saw a white horse who had a bow, a crown was given him, he went forth conquering and to conquer.

The **second seal** there went out a red horse, he was given power to take peace from the earth and to kill one another and unto him were given was a great sword. The third seal. I beheld a black horse, he that sat on him had a pair of balances in his hand. The third seal, John said, I heard a voice in the midst of the beast saying a measure of wheat for a penny and three measure of barley for a penny, and see that you hurt not the wine nor the oil

The **fourth seal**, John said, I saw a pale horse; his name was death and hell followed and power was given to him over the forth part of the earth to kill with the sword and with hunger and with death, and with the beast of the earth.

John said, when he opened the **fifth seal**, I saw under the alter the souls of them that was slain for the word of God, and for the testimony which they held: John saw white robes were given to those who were slain.

When he opened the **sixth seal,** there was a great earth quake, the sun became black as sack cloth of hair, and the moon became as blood; as the stars of heaven fell to the earth and the heaven departed as a scroll and every mountain and island were moved out of their places.

And the kings of the earth, and every great man, and the rich man, and the chief captains and the mighty man, and every bond man, and every free man, hid themselves in the dens and in the rocks of the mountains; and said to the mountain fall on us, and hide us from the face of him that sit on the throne, and from the wrath of the lamb: for the great day of his wrath has come; and who shall be able to stand.

Revelation 7, and I saw four angels standing on the four corners of the earth, holding the four winds of the earth, that the winds should not blow on the earth nor on the sea nor on any tree.

I saw another angel coming from the east having the seal of the living God, and he cried to the four angels to whom it was given to hurt the earth and the sea, saying, hurt not the earth nor the sea nor the trees till we have sealed the servants of our God in their four heads the number of them that were sealed an hundred and forty four thousand of all the trial of the children of Israel.

Matt, and he shall send his angels with the sound of a trumpet and they shall gather together his elect from the four winds from one end of heaven to the other.

THE SEVEN TRUMPETS

Revelation 8, when he opens the seal

When he opened the seven seal there was silence in heaven for the space of an hour; and I saw another angel came and stood at the alter having a gold censer; and there were given to him much incense, that he should offer it with prayer of all saints upon the golden alter which was before the throne. And the smoke of the incense, which came with the prayers of the saints, ascended up before God out of the angel's hands. And the angel took the censer and filled it with fire of the alter and cast it into the earth: and there were voices, and thunder and lightning and an earthquake. **The seven angles which stood before God were given seven trumpets; the seven trumpets prepared themselves to sound.**

The First angel sounded

Followed hail and fire mingled with blood, and they were cast upon the earth: and the third part of the trees were burnt up, and all green grass was burnt up.

The Second angle sounded

And it was a great mountain burning with fire was cast into the sea: And the third part of the sea became blood; and the third part of the creatures, which in the sea died; and the third part of the ships were destroyed.

And the third part of the creatures which was in the sea died and the third of the ship were destroyed.

The Third angel sounded

And there fell a great star from heaven, burning as if it was a lamp, and it fell upon the third part rivers, and upon the fountain of water; and the name of the star is called wormwood: and the third part of the water became wormwood, and many men died of the water because they were made bitter.

The Fourth Angle Sounded

And the third part of the sun was smitten, and the third part of the moon and the third part of the stars; the third part of them were darkened, the day shone not for a part of it, and the night likewise. And I beheld an angles flying though the midst of heaven, saying in a loud voice woe, woe, woe, to the inhabit of the earth by reason of the other voices of the trumpet of three angles, which are yet to sound.

The Fifth angle sounded
Revelation 9

A star fell from heaven unto the earth: and to him was given the key to the bottomless pit. And he opened the bottomless pit; and there arose a smoke out of the pit as the smoke of a great furnace; and the sun and the air was darkened by reason of the smoke of the pit. And there came out of the smoke locusts upon the earth: and unto them were given power, as the scorpions of the earth have power.

And to them it was given that they should not kill them, but they should be tormented five months: and their torment was that of a scorpion, when he strike a man, and in those days men shall seek death and shall not find it; and shall desire to die, but death shall flee from them. That they should not hurt the grass of the earth, neither any green thing, neither any tree; but only those men which have not the seal of God in therefore heads.

They were commanded not to kill them but to torture them five months. In those days men will seek to die but death will flee from them.

Shapes Of the locusts

The shape of the locusts were like unto horses prepared unto battle, and on their heads were as if it were crowns of gold, and their faces as the faces of men. And they had hair as the hair of a woman, their teeth were as teeth of a lion; and they had breath plates, as it were breast plates of iron; and the sound of their wing was the chariot of many horses running to battle. They had tails like unto scorpions and there were stings in their tails.

King Over them

And they had a king over them, which is the angles of the bottomless pit whose name in Hebrew tongue is A-bad-don, but in Greek tongue Satan's name is A-poll-on.

The Sixth Angles sounded

I John heard a voice from the fore horns of the golden alter which is before God, saying to the six angel which had the trumpet, loose the four angles which are bounded in the great Euphrates and the four angels were loosed which was prepared for an hour, and a day, and a month, and a year, for to slay the third part of man. And the number of the army of the horse were two hundred thousand thousands. And I John Saw horses, those who sat on them having breastplate of fire and out of there mouth came smoke, fire and brimstone. The men who were not killed by these plagues yet repented not.

GOD TWO WITNESSES

Revelation Cha.11

And I will give power to my witnesses and they shall prophesy a thousand two hundred and three score days cloth in sackcloth. These are the two olive trees, and the two candle sticks standing before the God of the earth. And if any man will hurt them, he must in this manner be killed. These have power to shut heaven, that it rained not in the days of their prophecy and have power over the water to turn them to blood and to smite the earth with plagues as often as they will. And when they have finished their testimony, the beast ascended out of bottle less pit shall make war with them and kill them and when they shall have finished their testimony, the beast that ascended out of the bottomless pit shall make war with them and kill them.

And their dead bodies shall lie in the street of the great city where Spiritually Sodom and Egypt where Christ was crucified. And the people and tongues and nations shall see their dead bodies three days and a half and their dead bodies shall not be put in the graves

And they that dwell upon the earth shall rejoice over them and make merry, and shall send gifts to one another; because these two prophets tormented them that dwell on the earth after three days and an half the spirit of God entered into them, and they stood upon their feet, and great fear fell upon them that saw them. And they heard a great voice from heaven, come up hither, and they ascended up to heaven in a cloud and their enemies beheld them. **The two are witnesses Are Moses And Elijah.** Elijah prophesied there shall not be dew nor rain.

1 King 17:1 +7. And Moses smite with the rod in his hand, and the waters in the rivers turned to blood. Exodus 7:17. the olive trees and the two candlesticks standing before God of the earth are Moses and Elijah, Revelation,11:3-6.

And at the same hour was there a great earthquake, in the earthquake seven thousand men was slain, the city were affrighted, and gave glory to God in heaven. And there were great voices in heaven, saying the kingdom of this world are become the kingdom of our Lord and of his Christ; and he shall reign forever and ever Revelation 11: 15. And the four and twenty elders, which sat before God on their seats fell upon their faces and worshiped God, saying, we give thee thanks O Lord God almighty which art, and was and are to come, because thy hast taken to thee thy great power, and has reigned.

Rev. 11: 18, Thy shall give rewards to the servant the prophets and to the saints and them that fear my name small and great; and should destroy them that destroy the earth.

The beast was taken and with him the false prophets that wrought miracles before him which he deceived all who had received the mark of the beast and them that worshiped his image these both were cast alive into a lake of fire burning with fire and brimstone, Rev. 20.

John said I saw another angle come down from heaven having the key of the bottomless pit and a great chain in his hand, and he laid hold on the dragon, that old serpent, which is the devil, and Satan, and bound him for a thousand years, and cast him into the bottomless pit and shut him up and set a seal upon him.

Verse 15, and whosoever was not written in the book of life was cast into the lake of fire. Rev. 19:5, and a voice came out of the throne saying, praise our God, all ye his saints, and ye who fear him, both small and great. John said and I heard as it was the voice of a great multitude, and as the voice of many waters, and as the voice of mighty thundering, saying al-le-Lu I—a, for the Lord God omnipotent reigneth, let us be glad and rejoice and give honor to his name, we are the brides of Christ, God is preparing his bride for his coming.

The marriage of the lamb is come and his bride has made herself ready, and to her was granted that she should arrayed in finen clean and white. for the fine linen is the righteous of the saints, John said he said unto me, these are the true saying of God. Rev. 22:7, behold I come quickly blessed is he that keepeth the sayings of the prophecy of this book. Verse 12, and behold I come quickly and my reward is with me to give every man according to his work shall be. I am Alpha and Omega the beginning and the end, the first and the last.

Blessed are those who do his commandments. That they may have the right to the tree of life, and may enter into the gates to the city. But outside are dogs, sorcerers, sexually immoral, murderers, and Idolaters and whosoever practices a lie. Jesus has sent my angels to testify to you these things in the churches. I am the root of David, the Bright and Morning Star. And the spirit and the bride say, come and let him, who thirsts come. Whosoever desire let Him take the water freely. Surly I am coming quickly.

The Vials of Wrath
Revelation Cha 15

And I John saw another sign in heaven, seven angels having the last plagues; for in them is filled up the wrath of God. And I saw as it were a sea of glass mingled with fire: and those who had gotten the victory over the beast, and over his image, and over his mark, and over the number of his name, stand on the sea of glass, having the harps of God and they sang the songs of Moses the servant of God and the song of the lamb saying. Great and marvelous are thy works Lord God thy mighty:

Who shall not fear thee and the glory of thy name? for only thy are holy. The temple of the tabernacle testimony was open: And the seven angels came out of the temple having the seven plagues cloth in pure and white linen.

And one of the four gave the seven angels seven golden vials full of the wrath of God, no man was able to enter into the temple, till the seven plagues of the seven angels were fulfilled. I heard a voice out of the temple saying to the seven angels go your way and pour out the vial upon.

The first angel went and poured his vial upon the earth and, there fell a noisome grievous sore upon the men which had the mark of the beast and upon them that worshiped his image.

The second angel poured out his vial upon the sea, and it became as blood of a dead man: and every living soul died in the sea. And the third angels poured out his vial upon the rivers and fountains of waters and they became blood. For they have shed the blood of the saint and prophets. And thy has given them blood to drink. Thy are righteous thy Judged.

The third angel poured out his bowl on the river and springs of waters, and they became blood. And I heard the angels of the waters saying: you are righteous O Lord. The one who is and who was and who is to be, because you have Judged these things, for they have shed the blood of the saints and prophets, and you have given them blood to drink for it is their just due.

The fourth angel poured out his vial out up on the sun, men was scorch with fire. They blasphemed the name of God and they repented not.

The fifth angel poured out his vial upon the seat of the beast; and his kingdom was full of darkness; and they gnawed their tongues for pain, and blasphemed the God because if their pain and their sores and repented not of their deeds.

The six angel poured out his vial upon the great river Euphrates and the water dried up. That the way of kings of the east be prepared and I saw three unclean spirits, like frogs coming out of the mouth of the dragon, out of the mouth of the beast, and out of the mouth of the false prophet.

They are spirits of demons, performing signs which go out to the kings of the earth and of the whole world, to gather them to the battle of that great day of God almighty.

And the seventh angel poured his vial into the air and there came a great voice out of the temple of heaven from the throne saying it is done.

And there were voices and thunders and lightning; and there were a Great earthquake. Such as was not since men were upon the earth, so mighty an earthquake, and so great. And the great city was divided into three parts. And the cities of the nation fell, and great Babylon came in remembrance before God to give unto her the cup of the wind of fierceness of his wrath. And the island fled away, and the mountains were not found. And there fell upon men a great hail out of heaven. Every stone about the weight of a talent and men blasphemed God because of the hail, for the plague was exceeding great. John said, showed him the Judgment, mystery, Babylon great, mother of Harlots.

BABYLON HAS FALLEN

Revelation Cha 18

The ten horns hate the whore and shall make her desolate and naked, and shall eat her flesh, and burn her with fire. For God has put in their Heart to full his will, and to agree, and give their kingdom to the beast until the words of God shall be fulfilled. And the woman which thy saw is the great city which reign over the kings of the earth. John I saw an angel come down from heaven who had great power and was lightened with his glory.

The angel cried out, saying Babylon the great is fallen, and it become the habitation of the devils, and the hold of every foul unclean hateful bird, for all nations have drunk of the wine of the wrath of her fornication. The king of the earth has committed fornication with her and the merchants of the earth are waxed rich though the abundance of her delicacies.

And I heard another voice from heaven saying, come out of her, my people that not partakers of her sins, and that ye receive not her plagues for her sin have reached heaven, and God has remember her iniquities. Reward her even as she rewarded you, and double unto her double. According to her works in the cup which she hath filled fill to her double. How much she has glorified herself. And lived deliciously, so much torment and sorry give her: for she said in her heart, sit I, a queen, an am no widow, and shall see no sorry, Therefore shall her plague come in one day, death and morning and she shall be utterly burned with fire: for strong is the Lord God who Judge her. That great city Babylon, that mighty city! For in one hour is thy judgment, the merchants shall weep and morn over her; for no man buy their merchandise anymore.

Revelation18, The merchandise of gold, silver, precious stones, pearls, fine linen purple and silk, scarlet, all the wonderful and beautiful things that thy soul lust after, all things that were dainty and goodly are departed from thee, and thy shall find them no more.

The merchants of these things, which was made rich by her, shall stand far off for the fear of torment, weeping and walling. For in one hour so great riches has gone from you.

Every shipmaster, and all the companies in ships, and sailors, and as many as trade by sea, stood afar off. And cried when they saw the smoke of her burning, saying what city is like this great city. rejoice over her, thou heaven and ye holy apostles and prophets; for God has revenged you on her and the might angel took up a stone like a millstone, and cast it into the sea, saying, thus with violence shall that great city Babylon be throne down, and shall be found no more at all.

And the voice of the harpers, and musicians, and of pipers, and trumpeters, shall be heard no more at all in thee: and no craftsman of whatever craft he be, shall be found any more in thee and the sound of the millstone shall be heard no more at all in thee, And the light of a candle shall shine no more at all in thee.

Ant the voice of the bridegroom shall be heard no more at all in thee: For thy merchants were the great men of the earth; for by their sorceries were all nations deceived. And in her was found the blood of the prophets, and of the saints, and all that were slain upon the earth.

The Tree Of Life

Blessed are they that do his commanded that they may have the right to the tree of life. Rev, 2: 7, to him who overcome, I will give to him to eat of the tree of life, which is in the mist of the paradise of God and may enter in though the gates into the city.

God's highway

Isaiah 35:8, and an highway shall be there, and a way, and it shall be called the way of holiness. The unclean shall not pass over it, but it shall be for those the wayfaring men, though fools shall not err therein. Holiness is your guide and shall lead you to the straight gate and the narrow way which will lead you to life, and you shall enter into the though the gates into the city.

Ps.97:4-6, His lighting enlighten the world The earth saw and trembled. The hills melted like wax at the presence of the Lord of the whole earth. The heavens declare his righteousness, and all the people see his glory.

The glory of the Lord shall endure forever. Matthew 16: 27, For the Son of man shall come in the glory of his father with his angles and then he shall reward every man according to his work. Matthew 19: 28, Jesus said unto them, I say unto you, that ye which have followed me, in the regeneration when the Son of man shall sit in the throne of his glory, ye also shall sit upon twelve throne Judging the twelve tribes of Israel.

Rev 21, John said, I saw a new heaven and a new earth for the first heaven and the new earth were passed away there were no more sea, and I John saw the holy city, new Jerusalem, coming down from God out of Heaven prepared as a bride adorned for her husband. And I heard a great voice out of heaven, saying the tabernacle of God is with men, and he will dwell with them and they shall be his people and himself shall be their God

He shall wipe away all tears from their eyes, there will be no more tears there will be no more death, no more sorry, there will be no more pain: for the formal things are passed away, Behold I make all things new. The fearful and the unbelievable and the abominable, the murderers, whoremongers, sorcerers, idolaters and all liars, shall have their part in the lake of fire which burn with fire brimstone which is the second death. Rev. 22:11, he that is holy let him be holy still, he that is just let him be Just still, he that is filthy let him be filthy still, he that is righteous let him be righteous still, he that is holy let him be holy still. John said, and I and I heard a great voice out of heaven saying, behold, the tabernacle of God is with men, and he will dwell with them, and they shall be his people, and God himself shall be with them, and be there God.

The Straight Gate

Matthew 7:13, enter ye in at the straight gate for wide is the gate and broad is the way, that lead to destruction, and many there be which go in thereat because straight is the gate and narrow is the way which lead to life and few there be that find it.

DESCRIPTION OF HEAVEN

Revelation 21: 10-26

John said God took him into a high mountain and showed him the great city. Heaven having the glory of God as her light was like unto a most precious stone, like a Jasper stone clear as crystal

The walls were great and high, the city has twelve gates, at the gate were twelve angels, the names of the twelve tribe of the children Israel were written on the gates.

The walls of the city had twelve foundations and in them were the names of the twelve apostles of the lamb of God.

The building of the wall was of Jasper, and the city pure gold like unto glass.

The foundation of the wall of the city were garnished with all matters precious stones. The first foundation was jasper, sapphire; a chalcedony; an emerald; a sardonyx, sardonyx, hyalite, beryl, a topaz, a jacinth, an jacinth.

The Twelve Gates had twelve Pearls, every several gate was of one Pearl and the streets of the city was pure gold, as it was transparent glass.

John said and I saw no temple therein: for the Lord almighty and the Lamb are the temple of it. And the city had no need of the sun, neither of the moon, to shine in it, for the glory of God did light, and the lamb is the light thereof. and the nation of them which are saved shall walk in the light of it: and the kings of the earth do bring their glory and honor into it.

And the gates of it shall not be shut at all by day. for there shall be no night there.

Rev. Cha. 22: 1-9, John saw a pure river of water of life, clear as crystal proceeding out of the throne of God and of the lamb, in the midst of the street of it and on each side of the river was there the tree of life, which bear twelve manner of fruit, and yield her fruit every month: and the leaves of the tree were for the healing of the nation.

And there shall be no more curse: but the throne of God and the lamb shall be it, and his servants shall serve him.

Rev. 22:7, behold, I come quickly blessed is he that keep the saying of the prophecy of this book. Verse 12, and behold I come quickly my reward is with me to give every man according to his work shall be. Verse 20, surly I come quickly. Verse 20, The grace of our Lord Jesus Christ be with you all A-men

BATTLE AT ARMAGEDDON

Revelation 19: 19, and I saw the beast and the king of the earth and their armies, gather together to make war against he who sat on the horse and his army. I saw three unclean spirits like frogs come out of the mouth of the dragon, and out of the mouth of the beast, and out of the mouth of the false prophet. For these are the spirits of the devil, working miracle which go forth unto the kings of the earth and of the whole world to gather them to the battle of the great day God almighty. And gather them into a place called Armageddon. Revelation 17:11-16, the ten horn and the ten kings shall have one mind. These make war with the lamb, and the lamb shall overcome them: for he is Lord of Lord and king of kings: and they that are with him are called chosen and faithful.

John said, and I saw heaven open a white horse and he who sat on it was called Faithful and true, he do judge and make war. His eyes were as of a flame of fire and on his head was many crowns and he had a name written, that no man knew, but he himself. And he was clothed with vesture dipped in blood: and his name is the word of God.

The armies which was in heaven followed him on white horses, cloth in fine linen white and clean. and out of his mouth go. A shard sword, that with it he should smite the nations: and he shall rule them with a rod of iron: which is the righiousness of God And the spirit and the bride say, come and let him that hear say, come and let him take the water of life freely. He who testify these things said surly I come quickly: and he has on his vesture And his thigh, a name written king of kings and Lord of Lords. We are the army of the Lord, we will participate in the warfare of Armageddon, we shall come back with Jesus riding white horses during the time of the battle of Armageddon.

Revelation 7:2-4, saw another angel having the seal of the living God and cried out, hurt not the earth nor the sea nor the trees till we have sealed the servant of our God in their fore head.

The number of them sealed were one hundred forty four thousand of the tribes of the children of Israel, a great number no man could number, of all nations and kindred and people and tongues stood before the throne and before the lamb cloth with white robes and palms in their hands and they worshiped God, saying, A-men, blessing and glory and thanks giving, and honor and power and thanks be unto our God forever and ever amen.

V-13, who are these arrayed in white robes? They came out of great tribulation and have washed their robes in the blood of the lamb. One hundred and forty four thousand Jews, Tribes Of Israel will go though the tribulation: they will not be harmed: Rev.7,. John saw a great multitude, which no man could number, of all nations, kindred, and people and tongues stood before the throne and before the lamb cloth with white robes and palms in their hands, salvation to our God.

DIFFERENCE BETWEEN
THESE AND THOSE

We are those in Rev. 3: 10. We are kelp out of the tribulation, we will be clothed in white raiment, we will sit with Jesus in his throne, we will wear crowns, we will sing new song. Revelation3: 5, We shall be cloth in white raiment, 3: 12, God shall make us a pillar in the temple of God Jesus will write upon us the name of God and the name of the city of God. Jesus will write upon us his new name.

Revelation 7: 13+14+ 15, These went though the tribulation and came out of the great tribulation, these are all Jews. These stand before the throne, these does not wear crowns, these serve God day and night. These are sealed during the first part of the tribulation, and are saved during the last part of the tribulation: These shall be priest of God and Christ during that time. Here we see a merciful God. Although the tribulation is a time of judgment it will be a time of salvation for the Jews.

Some one may say, if the multitude is saved during the tribulation I have time, wrong, no one who hears the gospel and reject it will have an opportunity to be saved during the tribulation

2 Thessalonians 10-12 and to all deceivableness of unrighteousness in them that perish; because they receive not the love of truth that they might be saved, and for this cause God send then a strong delusion that may believe a lie that they all might be damned who believe not the truth but had pleasure in unrighteousness.

Revelation 3: 5, he who over come shall be cloth in white raiment and I will not blot his name out of the book of life but I will confess his name before my father, and before the angels.

Matthew 19: 28, and Jesus unto his disciples, verily I say unto you who has followed me in this generation, when the son of man shall sit in the throne of his glory you shall sit upon twelve thrones judging the twelve tribes of Israel. We the disciples of Jesus shall sit upon the throne judging the twelve the tribes of Israel.

You are they who have continued with me in my temptation, I appoint you a kingdom as my father appointed unto me, that you may eat and drink at my table in my kingdom, and sit on thrones judging the twelve tribes of Israel, Luke 22: 28-29.

John said, I heard a voice of much people in heaven saying halleluiah Salvation, and glory, and honor, and power,unto the Lord our God, for true and righteousness is his judgment for he has judged the great whore which did corrupt the earth with her fornication and hath revenged the blood of his servants at her hands, hal-le-lu-ia. Rev. Cha. 19.

HEAVEN IS BUSY

And the four and twenty elders and the four beasts fell down and worshipped and sat on the throne saying Amen hal-le-lu-ia John said I heard a voice came out of heaven sayinbg, praise our God all ye his servants, and ye who fear him, both small and great And I heard as it was a voice of a great multitude and as the voice of many waters and as a voice of mighty thundering saying Hal-le-lu-ia For the Lord God omnipotent reigned let us be glad and rejoice and give honor to him. for the marriage of the lamb has come and her wife has made herself ready, and to her was granted that she should be arrayed in fine linen, clean and white: For the fine linen is the righteousness of saints.

Rev. 20: 4, John said I saw throne and they that sat upon them and judgment was given them and I saw for the witness the souls of them that were beheaded for the witness of Jesus and for the word of God and which had not worshipped the beast, neither his image, neither had received his mark upon their forehead or in their hand, and they lived and reign with Christ for a thousand years. But the rest of the dead did not live again until the thousand years finished, this is the first resurrection, over the second has no power, but they shall be priest of God and of Christ, and shall reign with him a thousand years.

Rev. 20: 1 John saw an angle coming from heaven having the keys of the bottomless pit and a great chain in his hand and bound Satan for a thousand years shut him up and set a seal him: Verse 7,when the thousand years has expired Satan shall be loosed out of his prison and shall go out and deceive the nation which are in the four quarters of the earth. during the thousand years, we who are caught up in the first resurrection will be with Christ forever, but the rest of the dead lived not again until the thousand years were finished. This is the second resurrection. Blessed and holy is he that hath part in the first resurrection on the second death hath no power.

1 Thessalonians 4: 16, for the Lord himself

Shall descend from heaven with a shout, with the voice of the archangel and with the triump of God. And the dead in Christ shall rise first then we which are alive and remain shall be caught up together with them in the cloud to meet the Lord in the air **and shall we ever be with the Lord.** Rev. 19: 14,We shall return with Christ following him on white horses. The bible is based on faith, the word of God has been completed in heaven. John 13:30, Jesus said it is finishes the victory has been won Satan was defeated at Calvary. Ephesians 2: 6, The church is sitting in heavenly places in Christ Jesus. The fight is fixed, we win Satan lose. We have been destined to win. The church must learn to treat Satan as a defeated foe. Whenever you doubt God you give Satan victory.

I John saw the stars of heaven fall upon the earth, the heaven departed as a scroll when it is rolled together, every mountain and island was moved out of its places: The kings of the earth, the rich men, the great men, the chief captains and the mighty men every bond man every free man hid themselves in the dens and in the rocks of the mountains; and said to the mountains fall on us, and hide us from the face of him that sit on the throne and from the wrath of the lamb: For the great day of the wrath has come, and who shall be able to stand. There is no human on the earth will be able to stand the wrath of God

Rev. 8:10, John said, I saw a mighty angel come down from heaven, cloth with a cloud and a rainbow was upon his head and his face was as it were the sun, his feet as pillars of fire, and he had in his hand a little book open and he sat his right feet upon the sea, and his left feet on the earth, and cried with a loud voice, as when a lion roar and when he had cried seven thunders had uttered their voices and when the seven thunders had uttered their voices John saw the seven thunders had uttered their voices and he said I was about to write and I heard a voice from heaven saying unto me seal up those things which the seven thundered uttered and write them not and the angels which I saw stand upon the sea and upon the earth Lifted up his hand to heaven and swear by him that liveth forever and ever, who created heaven and the things that are in the earth and in the sea and the things which are. **shall time be no more.** At this point the warfare will be over.

Verse 7, But in the days of the voice of **the seventh angels, when he shall begin to sound the mystery of God shall be finished,** as he has declared to his servants, the prophets. And the voice which I heard from heaven spoke to me again and said, go and take the little book which is open in the hand of the angel which stand upon the sea and upon the earth. John said, I went unto the angel and said unto him, give me the little book, and he said unto me take it and eat it up, and it shall make thy belly bitter, but it shall be in thy mouth sweet as honey, and I took the little book out of the angels hand, and ate it up and it was in my mouth sweet as honey as soon as I had eaten it my belly was bitter, and he said unto me thou must prophesy again before many people and nations and tongues.

Do not let it be said to late, the clock is ticking, the stage has been set. The action that is about to take place is not an entertainment moment but a time of Judgment. Matthew 7:10, Jesus to those who followed, assuredly, I say to you, I have not found such great faith, not even in Israel! and I say to you that many will come from east and west and sit down withAbraham, Isaac, and Jacob in the Kingdom of heaven.

But the sons of the kingdom will be cast into outer darkness. There will be weeping and gnashing of teeth. These are the children of the kingdom: then he said to another, follow me. But he said, Lord, let me first go and bury my father, Jesus said to him, let the dead bury their own, but you go and preach the kingdom of God.

And another said, Lord I will follow you, but let me first go and bid them farewell who are in my house.

Jesus said to him, no one having put his hands to the plow, and looking back, is fit for the kingdom of God. These are the children of the kingdom: this group made a vile to God, they started out with God but turned back; God said they will be cast out into outer darkness.

God is merciful he is giving you time to come inside the door. Noel preached forty days, it's going to rain, the warning was ignored, The people were destroyed because they rejected God's warning.

John preached as one crying in the wilderness, the kingdom of heaven is at hand they ignored the warning. God has sent many of his prophet to warn the people. He also has sent me as his ambassador and his prophetess to warn the people, come into the house of the Lord, Jesus is coming for his people those whom has made themselves ready and we shall be caught up to meet him in the air. Those who reject Christ will fill his wrath.

THIS IS THE LAST CALL.
THE LAST WARNING

This is not a rehearsal this is the real thing, Jesus is coming. John preached, Noel warn the people, they ignored him, the flood came, they were destroyed. the prophets are sending warnings, the pastors are preaching, The teachers are teaching, the witnesses are witnessing, preaching on the television, preaching on the radio, teaching from the word of God, you have no excuse. God is saying no excuse. don't let it be said too late. don't be left behind, don't take the example of the foolish virgins, Matt. 25, they were too late, they went out to buy but when they returned the door had been shut. When God shut a door no man can open it.

JESUS IS TALKING

And behold I come quickly: and my reward is with me, to give every man according as his work shall be. I am Alpha and Omega, the beginning and the end, the first and the last. Blessed are they that do his commandments, that they may have the right to the tree of life, and may enter in though the gates into the city, for without are dogs, and sorcerers, and whoremongers and murders, and idolaters and whosoever love and make a lie.

I Jesus have sent mine angel to testify unto you these things in the churches. I am the root and the offspring of David, and the bright and morning star. And the spirit and the bride say, Come. And let him that hear say, Come, and whosoever will, let him take the water of life freely.

For I testify unto every man that hear the word of the prophecy of this book, if any man shall add unto these things, God shall add unto him the plagues that are written in this book: And if any man shall take away from the word of the book of this prophecy, God shall take away his part out of the book of life, and out of the holy city, and from the things which are written in this book. He which testify these things said, Surely I come quickly, A—men, Even so come Lord Jesus. The grace of our Lord Jesus Christ be with you all A-men.